40-
Bible
Adventure

A Fascinating Journey to
Understanding God's Word

Christopher D. Hudson

BARBOUR
PUBLISHING

© 2011 by Barbour Publishing, Inc.

ISBN 978-1-61626-007-1

Produced with the assistance of Hudson & Associates. Special thanks to editorial assistants Jonathan Dunn and Melanie Holland.

The "Setting Up the Story," "Critical Observation," "Insight," and "Take It Home" sections have been adapted from Barbour's QuickNotes Simplified Commentary Series. Used with permission.

Unless otherwise noted, scripture quotations are taken from the King James Version of the Bible.

Scripture quotations marked NIV are taken from the HOLY BIBLE, NEW INTERNATIONAL VERSION®. NIV®. Copyright © 1973, 1978, 1984 by International Bible Society. Used by permission of Zondervan. All rights reserved.

Published by Barbour Publishing, Inc., P.O. Box 719, Uhrichsville, Ohio 44683, www.barbourbooks.com

Our mission is to publish and distribute inspirational products offering exceptional value and biblical encouragement to the masses.

ecpa Member of the
Evangelical Christian
Publishers Association

Printed in the United States of America.

For Dad and Mom

Thank you for first introducing me to the Bible

Contents

Introduction

While the Bible can change lives, understanding God's Word can be a challenge. The Bible is unlike most books we read—it's older, longer, and more involved. The book we call the Bible is actually an anthology of sixty-six separate books written over the course of fifteen hundred years.

Once you begin reading, however, you may find the Bible is far less confusing than you had feared. Each individual Bible book contributes to a larger story line that speaks of God's unending love for His people. The more familiar you are with the flow of the story, the more you'll get out of your Bible.

The 40-Day Bible Adventure can help you understand God's Word. Each chapter of this book is designed to aid in your journey of better understanding God's message for you. Commit to forty days, for about fifteen minutes each day, and you'll develop a basic understanding of scripture and be encouraged to better engage the Bible text.

Go ahead and turn the page—a rewarding adventure awaits.

DAY 1
CREATION

SETTING UP THE STORY

The Bible opens with the story of creation found in the book of Genesis. This story serves two primary purposes: First, it identifies God as the Creator of the world. Second, it explains the origin of all things. Everything is created by God according to His sovereign power.

If you have time, read the whole story: Genesis 1:1–2:25

GOD FORMS THE EARTH
Read Genesis 1:1–13
What is God's initial response to His creation?

_____

_____

_____

Insight
The original audience for this story would have been the people of God who lived during the time of Moses. Since they would already have been people of faith—people who knew the Lord—the story of creation is not so much an apologetic meant to convince unbelievers as it is a declaration of the mysterious wonder and grandeur of creation. These initial chapters are not intended to give a scientific account of creation but rather tell a story that highlights the powerful facts that God created this world and it exists within His control.

GOD FILLS THE EARTH
Read Genesis 1:14–25

Days 1–6 have literary parallels. How does day 1 parallel with day 4, day 2 with day 5, and day 3 with day 6?

_____

_____

_____

GOD CREATES MAN
Read Genesis 1:26–2:3

What were God's original intentions for humanity?

_____

_____

_____

Critical Observation

It is essential to understand the importance of God's blessing in Genesis 1:28. In fact, throughout the remainder of the book of Genesis, blessing remains a central theme. It denotes all that contributes to living fully as God intended, according to His purposes. In this case, the blessing relates to God's charge to "be fruitful, multiply." Interpreters generally recognize that command as given to Adam and Eve as the heads of the human race, not simply as individuals. In other words, God has not charged every human being with begetting children.

GOD CREATES WOMAN
Read Genesis 2:15–25

What do these verses teach us about man?

_____

_____

_____

What can you learn about God from this event?

_____

_____

_____

Insight

The word translated *helper* or *companion* does not refer to a servant. In fact, Jesus Christ uses the Greek equivalent of the word to describe the Holy Spirit, who would help believers after the Lord's ascension. It signifies the woman's essential contribution, not inadequacy. The description of this companion as "suitable" or "corresponding" suggests something that completes a polarity, like the North Pole corresponds to the South Pole.

Take It Home

It's possible that the naked condition of Adam and Eve as described at the close of Genesis 2 goes beyond a physical description. It also applies to the psychological unity and transparency required for a marriage relationship. Physically, they were naked and shared their bodies with each other; psychologically, they were not ashamed and hid nothing from each other. They were at ease without any fear of exploitation. While perfect relationships will not be achieved this side of heaven, through the power of Christ we can come closer to living in restored harmony with each other. What can you do to cultivate a proper openness and trust in your relationships, whether with your spouse, family, or friends?

Connecting the Story Line

- Genesis 1–2 reveals God's original intentions for the world and for humanity. We also learn that God has never intended for humans to live apart from Him or in conflict with each other. The Old Testament presents the unified nation of Israel; and in the New Testament (and today), we have the church, a community of believers with one Lord, Jesus Christ.

- God is sovereign and powerful, loving and caring. These important principles about God that show up time and again in the Bible are first presented in the creation account.

DAY 2
THE FALL

SETTING UP THE STORY

God greatly blesses Adam and Eve and gives them everything. They enjoy all the food they need, companionship with each other, and an intimate relationship with God. With all this blessing comes a single command: Do not eat from the tree of the knowledge of good and evil.

Sadly, at the beginning of chapter 3, Adam and Eve succumb to temptation and disobey God's command. Their resulting choice, known as "the Fall," introduces sin into the world. Along with sin also come fear, shame, insecurity, and judgment. Yet even in such a terrible story, seeds of hope and redemption can be found.

If you have time, read the whole story: Genesis 3:1–4:16

THE SERPENT'S TEMPTATION
Read Genesis 3:1–7
In what ways is the woman tempted? And the man?

_____
_____
_____

GOD'S JUDGMENTS
Read Genesis 3:8–20
How would you summarize God's judgments on the man and woman?

_____
_____
_____

Insight
Genesis 3:15 has traditionally been seen as the first prophecy about Jesus and His ultimate work to defeat Satan. The reference seems to pit Satan against the ultimate representative of perfect humanity, Jesus.

ADAM AND EVE ARE BANISHED FROM THE GARDEN
Read Genesis 3:21–24
What is different about Adam and Eve's life after the Fall?

_____

_____

_____

Critical Observation
Angels (often called *cherubim*) surround and symbolize God's presence in the Old Testament (Exodus 25:17–22; Ezekiel 10:15). Genesis 3:24 describes them protecting the tree of life with a flaming sword to keep humanity away. This is an apt picture of the separation established between God and His creation. Humanity is completely excluded, with no resources of their own to allow them to enter into God's paradise. It would take a divine act to bridge the gap.

THE RESULTS OF THE FALL SPREAD
Read Genesis 4:1–12
What seem to be the fundamental differences between Cain and Abel?

_____

_____

_____

Insight

Following Adam and Eve's departure from the garden, we see the consequences of sin play out in the fractured relationship of Cain and Abel, ultimately leading to Abel's murder. Such actions would have been unthinkable before—but as a result of the Fall, sin becomes commonplace.

Take It Home

Despite the blessings each of us might have in our own lives, it can be particularly easy to focus on the things we *don't* have instead. This was the temptation that the serpent offered Eve. Though God had given her everything she could need, Eve was still curious about the one thing she was denied—and her poor decision led to the entrance of sin and death into the world. To a lesser degree, we, too, are constantly tempted to focus on the things we don't have instead of the blessings God has already provided. Such poor focus not only keeps us from recognizing God's gifts and praising Him for them, but it can also lead to poor decision making and sin. Are there blessings from the Lord in your life? Do you have trouble recognizing them and giving thanks to God?

Connecting the Story Line

- Creation is damaged and distorted by the Fall. The rest of the Bible tells the story of God's plan to make things right and restore creation to His original intention.

- Sin damaged more than humanity's relationship with God—it also damaged people's ability to have perfect relationships with each other and affected the relationship between humanity and the created world.

- Examples of the effects of sin on creation include weeds, disease, earthquakes, hurricanes, and other kinds of disasters. Romans 8:19–22 tells us that the creation is also looking forward to being restored to its perfect state.

Day 3
Noah

Setting Up the Story

The impact of sin's introduction into the world continues. Genesis 6–8 covers the degradation of society and tells of Noah and his three sons, Shem, Ham, and Japheth. In chapter 6, the story is not too far removed from the creation account of Genesis 1. We can imagine how grieved God is that the people He created have already strayed so far. Yet God loves His creation and does not wish to see it all destroyed. The story of Noah is the story of God's plan to preserve the earth.

If you have time, read the whole story: Genesis 6–9

Before the Flood
Read Genesis 6:1–12
How would you describe the state of humanity during this time?

_____

_____

_____

Why do you think God is so grieved by humanity's wickedness?

_____

_____

_____

NOAH AND THE ARK
Read Genesis 6:13–22

What does this passage tell you about how God viewed His creation at this time?

_____

_____

_____

Critical Observation

Did Noah's ark hold over a billion species? Probably not. Keep in mind that the modern concept of species is not the same as the word *kind* in the Bible. There were likely several hundred different kinds of land animals that would have needed to be taken into the ark. The sea animals stayed in the sea, and many species could have survived in egg form. Noah could also have taken younger varieties of some larger animals. And, don't forget, the ark was a huge structure—the size of a modern ocean liner three stories high.

THE FLOOD
Read Genesis 7:11–24

What is the hope you can still find in this story?

_____

_____

_____

Insight

The account of the floodwaters covering the earth is both majestic and terrible. In many ways, the story is reminiscent of the creation account. Like Genesis 1, the story of the flood is structured by a careful counting of the days (371 in all).

AFTER THE RAIN
Read Genesis 8:1–12
What do you think the dove symbolizes?

_____

_____

_____

THE RESULTS OF THE FLOOD
Read Genesis 8:13–9:3; 9:12–17
What does God's promise and blessing tell you about God's relationship with humanity?

_____

_____

_____

Insight
The Hebrew word for *rainbow* is also the word for a battle bow. God seems to be saying that His bow is now put away, hung in place by the clouds, and the storm is over. As a result, whenever clouds appear over the earth and a rainbow appears, God will remember His covenant and His people will remember His promise.

Which of Noah's character traits should you consider emulating?

_____

_____

_____

Take It Home
Noah's ark was a massive construction, and it could not have been built overnight. While Noah was working on it, he likely would have faced resistance and confusion from those around him, including his family. However, Noah stayed strong in his faith in God, and when the flood

came he was able to preserve his family and the creatures of the earth. Noah's story reminds us that it is possible to be right with God and continue in faith even when surrounded by wickedness and unbelief. Nowhere does God promise that such perseverance will be easy—but in His love and mercy He will always provide what we need. Our challenge is to listen to God in obedience, no matter our circumstances.

Connecting the Story Line

- The story of Noah reminds us that God takes sin very seriously.

- When He placed His rainbow in the sky, God renewed His everlasting covenant with His creation.

- From God's promise to preserve earth, we get the sense that human history is headed someplace specific. The story of the Bible traces that history from creation through the new heaven and new earth described in Revelation 20–22.

Day 4
Abraham

Setting Up the Story

Chapter 11 represents a third beginning in Genesis. The first was at creation, the second was at the flood, and the third is at the tower of Babel (read its story in Genesis 11). Yet beginning in chapter 12, we see God setting a new course for His people. God promises to bless the world through Abram's descendants.

If you have time, read the whole story: Genesis 12:1–20:18

God's Covenant with Abram
Read Genesis 15:1–7

God had previously promised to build the family of Abram (known later as Abraham) into a great nation. What motivates Abram's complaint to God in verses 2 and 3?

_____

_____

_____

What assurance does God offer to Abram?

_____

_____

_____

Critical Observation

Genesis 15:6 is sometimes considered one of the most important verses in the Old Testament. God declares Abram righteous and in good standing before Him on the basis of Abram's faith. His faith was "counted unto him for righteousness." While this connection between faith and righteousness is most often considered a New Testament concept, Genesis 15:6 confirms that God has always desired faith from His people. He cares more about a person's internal being than his external appearance. We later see this concept echoed in the prophets (see an example in Hosea 6:6) and throughout the New Testament.

HAGAR AND ISHMAEL
Read Genesis 16
What negative outcomes arise from Abram and Sarai's actions?

_____

_____

_____

Insight
When Abram slept with Hagar, he was following an accepted custom of the day. However, it also appears he was acting out of fear and unbelief. God had promised an heir, but Abram doubted God's ability to fulfill His promise and wanted to help it along. Abram did not yet know that God intended Isaac, not Ishmael, to be his true heir. The story stands as a reminder to trust God and His promises.

ABRAM BECOMES ABRAHAM
Read Genesis 17:1–8
In this story, God is about to renew and expand upon His promise to Abraham. What action does God require of him (see verse 1)?

_____

_____

_____

Why do you think God changes Abram's name?

_____

_____

_____

Insight

In the ancient Near East, to name someone or something was to claim it as one's own, like a father would name a child entering the family. When God changes Abram's name to Abraham (which means "father of a multitude"), He not only points to the future fulfillment of His promise but also claims Abraham as His own.

GOD PROMISES ABRAHAM AND SARAH A SON
Read Genesis 17:15–21

Why do you think Abraham laughs when God says he will have a son? Do you think it was wrong to laugh? Why or why not?

_____

_____

_____

Take It Home

Thirteen years pass between the end of Genesis 16 and the beginning of Genesis 17. During that time, Abraham likely believed that Ishmael would be his heir and Sarah would never bear him a son. He was not expecting a visit from the Lord, and he was not expecting God to fulfill His promise of an heir in their old age. Often God answers prayer and fulfills His promises in unexpected ways. Are you willing to be surprised by God? Do you have eyes to see Him work in unusual ways? Consider whether your expectations limit God, or whether you really believe that He is capable of working beyond anything we can ask or imagine (Ephesians 3:20).

Connecting the Story Line

- The covenant God makes with Abraham is the same one He upholds through the lives of Isaac, Jacob (Isaac's son), and hundreds of generations of the Israelites.

- From the beginning of the world, God planned to bless the world through one of Abraham's descendants: Jesus Christ (see Galatians 3:8).

Day 5
Isaac

Setting Up the Story
Abraham has a son named Isaac. Genesis 21–24 tells
the story of Isaac's birth, early life, and marriage. Isaac's
birth also marks the beginning of the fulfillment of one
of God's covenant promises: Abraham would become the
father of a great nation.

If you have time, read the whole story: Genesis 21:1–26:35

The Birth of Isaac
Read Genesis 21:1–7
What do the circumstances surrounding Isaac's birth tell
us about God and His ability to keep His word?

_____

_____

_____

Insight
Sarah's words in Genesis 21:6 refer to Genesis 18:11–12. It
was during this earlier time that Sarah had laughed at the
angels who had told her she would have a son. Sarah had a
difficult time believing in God's plan—but He performed a
miracle by giving her a child at such an advanced age.

An Offering
Read Genesis 22:1–18
Why do you think God tests Abraham like this? What is
accomplished?

_____

_____

_____

While we don't know how old Isaac is at this time, he is old enough to help carry the wood and ask an insightful question. What do you imagine is Isaac's response to the events that unfold?

_____

_____

_____

Insight
Abraham could not have offered Isaac without Isaac's consent. Remember that Isaac bore the wood up the mountain and was likely the stronger of the two. As a young man, he was also certainly faster. Though he would have been big enough and strong enough to resist his father, Isaac chose to be obedient to Abraham and to God.

ISAAC'S MARRIAGE
Read Genesis 24:1–51
Name some ways you see God at work in this story.

_____

_____

_____

Insight
A camel can consume up to twenty-five gallons of water in ten minutes. Consider that the servant had ten camels, and a typical water jar held about three gallons of water. Rebekah would have had to make many trips to the well, and her labors would have taken quite some time.

Critical Observation

The scene in Genesis 24:39–49, in which Abraham's servant seeks to obtain the approval of Rebekah's family, is filled with tension. In fact, Genesis 24 as a whole is an excellent example of ancient storytelling. People in the ancient Near East enjoyed repetition—actually, they preferred it—as they heard or read stories. The servant's repetition of details is an effective literary device deliberately employed by the author of Genesis.

The Bible's account of Isaac emphasizes a number of characters who exhibited obedience to God. Which episodes of obedience in Isaac's story are the most striking to you?

_____

_____

_____

Take It Home

Obedience to God is a matter of not only what you turn over to God—but also those aspects of your life you retain for yourself. Can God get close to the most important things in your life—your possessions, plans, dreams, and relationships? Sometimes the supreme test of our faith is a matter of putting obedience to God above something we have cherished all our lives. Sometimes it involves doing something that might seem foolish to others. Abraham, for example, could not understand why God was asking him to sacrifice Isaac, but he trusted the Lord and was willing to give up everything he had in service to God. Are you willing to obey God sacrificially in all areas of your life?

Connecting the Story Line

- God told Abraham that his descendants would be as numerous as the stars. His son Isaac is the first generation of the fulfillment of that promise.

- Isaac's birth was miraculous, given Sarah's age and inability to have children. It demonstrated God's power and ability to keep His promises, facts that God proves time and time again in scripture.

- Abraham's willingness to sacrifice his son provides another picture by which we can understand God's willingness to sacrifice Jesus on the cross.

DAY 6
JACOB

SETTING UP THE STORY

The entire book of Genesis emphasizes the sovereignty of God and the wisdom of His apparent "delays." Chapters 26–36 trace this sovereignty through the generation following Isaac. God's plan will always prevail, and the struggles faced by Isaac, his son (Jacob), and their families illustrate this principle.

If you have time, read the whole story: Genesis 25:19–36:43

JACOB AND ESAU
Read Genesis 25:19–34
In what ways are Jacob and Esau different?

_____

_____

_____

Insight
What is the birthright, and why does Jacob want it so badly? Deuteronomy 21:17 and 1 Chronicles 5:1–2 tell us that the birthright involves both a material and a spiritual blessing. The possessor of the birthright receives a double portion of the inheritance, and he also becomes the head of the family and spiritual leader after the passing of his father (Genesis 43:33). In the case of this family, the birthright also determines who will continue the covenant God made with Abraham.

JACOB GETS ISAAC'S BLESSING
Read Genesis 27:1–40
What does Isaac's blessing promise for Jacob?

_____

_____

_____

Critical Observation
The theme of the younger gaining honor over and against the older appears often in the Bible, including several instances specifically in the genealogy of Christ. Examples include Seth's lineage being chosen over Cain's lineage (Genesis 4:26–5:8), Isaac being chosen over Ishmael (Genesis 17:18–19), Rachel being chosen over Leah (Genesis 29:18), and Joseph being chosen over each of his older brothers (Genesis 37:3). This theme highlights God's sovereign and gracious plan for His people. None of those chosen ones were particularly deserving in the world's eyes; they did not have the natural rights of the firstborn. However, they were each called specifically by God. The genealogy of Christ did not come about by accident or natural consequence but was definitively designed by the Lord.

JACOB'S DREAM
Read Genesis 28:10–22
Why does Jacob erect a monument? What does it signify?

_____

_____

_____

JACOB'S MARRIAGE
Read Genesis 29:13–30

How might you contrast Jacob's and Laban's character traits?

_____

_____

_____

Insight

Is Jacob's story an argument in favor of polygamy? Not necessarily. It is a description of reality as it happened. Many other men in the Old Testament took multiple wives, including Kings David and Solomon, yet there is no indication anywhere in scripture that polygamy is God's intention for marriage. If anything, Jacob's story stands as an argument against multiple wives. Rachel and Leah are frequently in conflict over their shared husband. The practice brings trouble and discord to their lives.

JACOB'S FAMILY
Read Genesis 29:31–30:24

What recurring themes appear in this story? What significance do you think they have?

_____

_____

_____

JACOB WRESTLES WITH GOD
Read Genesis 32:22–32

What do you think is the significance of this story? What does it tell us about Jacob?

_____

_____

_____

Take It Home

Frequently in life, we encounter delays and obstacles that upset and inhibit our plans. In these moments, it can be difficult to trust God. *If He really knew what He was doing, why did I not succeed? Why am I still waiting?* We must remember that God's timing is not always our timing. Jacob worked seven years to win Rachel as his wife, yet his wish was denied. He was forced to labor seven more years to marry her. It would have been difficult to trust God's sovereignty, yet Rachel ultimately became his wife and the mother of Joseph, who would go on to rescue his family from starvation. God's plan prevailed. Have you experienced failure recently? In what ways are you waiting on God? What do you think He wants to teach you during this time?

Connecting the Story Line

- When Jacob wrestles with God, he is given a new name, *Israel* (Genesis 32), which will become the name for all those descended from Abraham, Isaac, and Jacob.

- Abraham's lineage and his covenant with the Lord continue through the descendants of Jacob. His children become the fathers of Israel's twelve tribes.

Day 7
Joseph and His Brothers

Setting Up the Story
The last fourteen chapters of Genesis describe Jacob's twelve sons, though most of the story focuses on Joseph. This whole section reveals how God's plan for His people triumphs over human frailties. God will guide and strengthen those who follow Him.

If you have time, read the whole story: Genesis 37–50

Joseph's Journey to Egypt
Read Genesis 37:3–36
List some reasons Joseph's brothers may have hated him.

_____

_____

_____

Insight
As a result of their hatred, Joseph's brothers sell him into slavery. They hide their actions from their father and lead him to believe he has been killed by wild animals.

Joseph's Success in Egypt
Read Genesis 39:1–41:57
In what ways does God turn Joseph's misfortunes into good?

_____

_____

_____

JOSEPH'S BROTHERS IN EGYPT
Read Genesis 42:1–38
What irony do you see in the story of Joseph's brothers' visit to Egypt?

_____

_____

_____

Critical Observation
The trip to Egypt was long (250–300 miles) and dangerous, and a round-trip could consume six weeks' time.

Throughout the course of Joseph's life, he has discerned God's providential control of events. Four times he states that God, not his brothers, is behind what has happened (Genesis 45:5, 7–9).

Joseph encourages his family to be completely honest with Pharaoh when asked about their occupation so that he will send them to live in Goshen (Genesis 46:34). Goshen had some of the best pastureland in all of Egypt. It would be a place to keep the Hebrews isolated and insulated from the culture and religion of Egypt, since the Egyptians considered sheep unclean and Hebrews detestable (Genesis 43:32).

JOSEPH TESTS HIS BROTHERS
Read Genesis 44:1–34
Why do you think Joseph tests his brothers?

_____

_____

_____

In what ways have Joseph's brothers changed since he has last seen them?

_____

_____

_____

Insight

Why does Joseph put his brothers through this test? Was it just an act of vengeance—the product of twenty years of bitterness and anger? No! The Bible is very clear that Joseph never indulges in any resentment against others who had injured him (Genesis 45:5; 50:18–21). Joseph's purpose in speaking harshly and accusing his brothers of spying is not motivated by bitterness but by a desire to covertly discover information regarding the health and well-being of his father, Jacob, and his younger brother, Benjamin. He also is testing their character: Have they changed in how they care for each other?

FATHER AND SON REUNITED

Read Genesis 46:1–30

In what ways does the story of Joseph have a happy ending?

_____

_____

_____

Take It Home

God is never defeated by anyone's deceit. Jacob deceived and was deceived. His sons hated, envied, plotted, and lied. And yet at the end of the chapter, God has placed Joseph exactly where he needs to be in order to accomplish God's purposes. All this points to the sovereignty of God. When we sin and go against the will of God, we don't thwart the purpose of God; we thwart ourselves. Our job is not to work out the details. Joseph didn't. Our job is to remain pure and usable. God will work out the details. He did in the case of Joseph, and He will do it for you, too.

Finally, Joseph is an excellent example to follow regarding life's disappointments. Nowhere in this narrative do we see Joseph feeling sorry for himself or blaming others. He simply took each situation as it came and made the best out of it. Frequently our biggest problem in life is thinking that having problems is a problem.

Connecting the Story Line

- Joseph saves his family, God's chosen people, from extinction by starvation.

- More specifically, Joseph saves the life of his brother Judah—who will become an ancestor of Jesus Christ (see Matthew 1:2–3).

- The journey of Joseph and his family to Egypt explains how Abraham could be given the Promised Land, though his descendants will still have a need to conquer it.

DAY 8
THE BIRTH AND EARLY LIFE OF MOSES

SETTING UP THE STORY

God's people had escaped starvation by moving to Egypt
during Joseph's lifetime. Since that time, the people have
become prosperous and numerous—too much so for
Pharaoh, who moves to enslave them. That's where the
story of Exodus 1 picks up.

If you have time, read the whole story: Exodus 1:1–4:17

A NEW KING'S POLICY
Read Exodus 1:8–22
What motivates Pharaoh's actions? What does he want to
prevent in regard to the Israelites?

_____

_____

_____

Insight

There are times in life when it appears God is silent. The
first chapter of Exodus is one such time. Yet as the story
of Moses' early life and eventual leadership of Israel demonstrates, God is always present and His hand is always
at work in the lives of His children. God's way and plan
are not always apparent, but He cares for His people and
keeps His promises. The story of Moses is an excellent illustration of this fact.

THE BIRTH OF MOSES
Read Exodus 2:1–10
How is God at work through the birth and adoption of Moses?

_____

_____

_____

MOSES FLEES TO MIDIAN
Read Exodus 2:11–25
What positive and negative traits of Moses does this story depict?

_____

_____

_____

Insight
Verse 11 passes over nearly forty years of Moses' life, picking up the story again in Moses' adulthood. Having been raised in Pharaoh's household, Moses is torn between his Jewish and Egyptian identities. However, as his actions make clear, Moses chooses to identify himself with his enslaved people, Israel.

THE BURNING BUSH
Read Exodus 3:1–14
List some of the different ways God identifies Himself to Moses. What is meaningful about each one?

_____

_____

_____

Critical Observation

Many people have attempted to explain the burning bush as something other than a miracle. Some say that it was a natural phenomenon called "St. Elmo's fire," a discharge of electricity that causes a kind of glow. Others say it may have been a volcanic phenomenon, a beam of sunlight piercing through a crack in the mountain, or a purely psychological experience. Moses himself, however, provides a wholly supernatural explanation—the burning bush that would not be consumed was aglow with the presence of the Lord.

Insight

Moses wants to prove that he is not the man for the task that God has given him. The essence of Moses' argument is, "Send someone else!" Yet deliverance will not be by Moses' strength and power. God has other plans that He will soon reveal.

SIGNS FOR MOSES
Read Exodus 4:1–12

Why do you think God performs these miracles for Moses? How does Moses respond?

_____

_____

_____

Take It Home

Too often we easily acknowledge the fallibility of those who do not know or serve God, while failing to recognize our own weaknesses and shortcomings. Having acknowledged the depravity of humanity in general, we should not also forget the fallibility of the faithful. Every detail of our lives, every incident, every failure, is employed by God providentially to further His purposes. While this should in no way make us lax in our desire to know God's will and obey Him, it should serve to assure us that even when we fail, He does not. How do you see this in your own journey? What can you learn from Moses' experiences, his victories, and his failures?

Connecting the Story Line

- God upholds His covenant with Abraham, Isaac, and Jacob by providing a deliverer who will lead His people out of slavery and back into the Promised Land (Genesis 12:1–7).

- Moses was a child born under miraculous circumstances, saved by the hand of God from a king who wanted to take his life. Thousands of years later, Jesus would also be born through God's providence and saved from a king who wished him dead. And just as Moses became a deliverer who rescued his people, so did Jesus. Moses is another biblical figure who anticipated the ultimate deliverance found in Christ.

Day 9
The Exodus from Egypt

Setting Up the Story
In Exodus 3 Moses encounters God in a burning bush
and receives instructions to return to Egypt and lead
the Israelites out of slavery (an event often called "the
Exodus"). Though Moses feels uncertain about his
mission and fears Pharaoh, he reluctantly obeys God.
After meeting stiff resistance from Pharaoh
and hopelessness from his fellow Israelites, Moses
witnesses the miraculous power of God, who brings
His people out of Egypt.

If you have time, read the whole story: Exodus 4:18–14:31

Moses' First Appeal to Pharaoh
Read Exodus 5:1–9
If you were in Moses' position, how would you feel after
hearing Pharaoh's response?

_____

_____

_____

God Promises Deliverance
Read Exodus 5:22–6:9
Why does God make this promise? What does it show
the Israelites?

_____

_____

_____

Insight

God's assurance of deliverance from slavery and the Israelites' establishment in the Promised Land looks back to one of His promises to Abraham (often called the Abrahamic covenant). However, even the promise of deliverance does little to raise the hopes of the downtrodden Israelites. It will take a more dramatic action from the Lord to bring His people out of Egypt.

THE PLAGUES
Read Exodus 7:8–11:30

What do you learn about God in that He discriminates between the Egyptians and the Israelites in several of the plagues?

_____

_____

_____

Which plagues do you think would have been the most devastating to the people of Egypt?

_____

_____

_____

Critical Observation

Several of the plagues can be seen as challenges, subtle or overt, to various Egyptian deities. Frogs, for example, were regarded as having divine power. The Egyptian goddess Heqet was portrayed as a woman with a frog's head. In addition, the plague of darkness challenged one of the most prominent Egyptian deities, the sun god Re, as well as Nut, the goddess of the sky. In this way, God demonstrated His power over all of creation. The plagues were an indictment on the gods of Egypt—they manifested God's existence and power.

THE PASSOVER
Read Exodus 12:21–30

What symbolism is shared between the Passover and Jesus' death on the cross?

_____

_____

_____

Insight

Both the Old and New Testaments use the image of a Passover lamb to describe Jesus' sacrifice on the cross. Indeed, at times He is specifically referred to as the Lamb of God (Exodus 12; Isaiah 53:7; John 1:29).

CROSSING THE RED SEA
Read Exodus 12:31–39; 14:5–31

What does Israel's final escape tell us about the Israelites, Pharaoh, and God?

_____

_____

_____

Take It Home

God's actual judgment on sin, as we saw in the plagues and the ultimate destruction of Pharaoh and his army in the Red Sea, is something that many people seek to deny. Judgment is not easy to believe in or dwell on. In addition, we often observe in the world the prosperity of the wicked and suffering of the righteous. It is natural to wonder where God is in such situations. The Exodus reminds us that God never forgets His people, and whether in the present or the future, He will put the world to right. We are called to trust in His sovereignty and justice by faith.

Connecting the Story Line

- God continues to uphold the covenant with His people by appearing to Moses as the God of his forefathers—Abraham, Isaac, and Jacob. He delivers His people from slavery, as promised, and guides them on their journey into the Promised Land.

- The Passover story provides a key lens through which we may view the sacrifice of Jesus, the Lamb of God.

- The Israelites' freedom from slavery and oppression illustrates the way God frees His people from sin and death. Romans 6 speaks of our being freed from slavery to sin.

Day 10
The Ten Commandments

Setting Up the Story
Exodus 19 serves as a preamble to the commandments
God gives to Israel while they are en route to the
Holy Land. Chapter 19 reveals the purpose of the Ten
Commandments, as well as the perspective we should
have toward them. These commandments (given in
Exodus 20) are one of the keys to understanding the Old
Testament and serve as the core of the entire set of laws
given through Moses. They set out God's law for His
people in broad strokes, outlining how we are to relate to
Him and honor His image in others.

If you have time, read the whole story:
Exodus 19:1–20:26; 32–34

At Mount Sinai
Read Exodus 19:1–8, 16–20
How might God's rescue of His people from Egypt have
prepared them for His commandments?

_____

_____

_____

Insight
Israel must keep God's covenant, defined by the law, to
maintain their blessing as God's people. Israel's calling
is a position of both privilege and responsibility. They
are given the commandments to distinguish themselves
from other nations, so that they will be able to fulfill their
priestly calling (Exodus 19:6).

THE TEN COMMANDMENTS
Read Exodus 20:1–17

How would you summarize these commandments in a sentence or two?

_____

_____

_____

Read Matthew 22:34–40

How do you see the Ten Commandments present in Jesus' words?

_____

_____

_____

Critical Observation

Jesus and the writers of the New Testament often seemed to disparage the law. But their opposition was not against the law but against those who abused the law in order to exercise power over others. These people set up a system of works that emphasized their own teaching rather than the heart of God. In order to refute their false teachings, Jesus and the apostles taught a proper perspective on the law. Paul says the law is provisional and preparatory, and is superseded by the new covenant. The law is good—but the new covenant in Christ is far better (Luke 11:45–52; Galatians 3:1–29; Hebrews 7:11–19).

THE GOLDEN CALF
Read Exodus 32:1–20

What does this incident tell us about Israel? In what ways do you think you are like or unlike them?

_____

_____

_____

Look back to Exodus 20. Which of the Ten Commandments are broken by this event?

_____

_____

_____

Insight
There is a cause-and-effect relationship between the absence of leadership and the practice of idolatry. While
Moses is gone for forty days and nights, receiving instructions to build the tabernacle, the Israelites use his absence
as a pretext to take immoral action, seizing the opportunity to create a false image of God.

THE NEW TABLETS
Read Exodus 34:1–10
Do you think the Israelites deserved God's forgiveness?
Why or why not?

_____

_____

_____

Take It Home
The law is a gracious provision for the nation of Israel,
albeit a temporary one. The new covenant would be far
better, but the old covenant is a necessary prerequisite
and preparation. In the first covenant, God's majesty and
might are manifested to all, but only a select few can draw
near. In the new covenant, all who wish can draw near, but
only a few behold His majesty.

    The first manifestation of God on Mount Sinai por-
trays the spectacular truth of the holiness of God and
the separation which that demands. It makes us aware of
our sinfulness and our inability to reach God's standards.
The second manifestation of the Lord on Mount Calvary

reveals the grace of God, by which we may draw near to Him. We must be careful to keep both the holiness and the grace of God in perspective.

Connecting the Story Line

- God reestablishes His covenant with the people of Israel. If they obey His commandments, He will protect them and lead them to the Promised Land.

- The Ten Commandments provide the basis for Jesus' moral teaching in the Gospels (the books of Matthew, Mark, Luke, and John).

- God's grace to Israel after the golden calf incident demonstrates the consistency of His character from the Old Testament to the New. He is always holy and righteous, but He is also always loving and merciful.

DAY 11
THE LAW

SETTING UP THE STORY
In Galatians 3 the apostle Paul teaches that God designed the law to shepherd His people until Christ came to earth. The law was never intended to be God's final answer to sin—that would be Jesus' role. Much of the law is concerned with the distinctions between clean and unclean, because the law sought to distinguish Israel from her pagan neighbors and keep her as a people holy and set apart for God's use. The people of Israel were always prone to stray from the Lord, but close observance of the law was designed to bring their focus back to God.

If you have time, read the whole story:
Leviticus–Deuteronomy

THE OFFERINGS
Read Leviticus 1:1–4; 2:1–3; 3:1–2; 4:1–3; 5:17–19
List the different kinds of sacrifices found in these verses. Why do you suppose there are different kinds of offerings?

Insight
God called the Israelites to sacrifice the best animals and crops they had. To make an offering was not without cost, but it was fitting to honor such a holy and mighty God with the best possessions a person had. These sacrifices reminded the people of their devotion to the Lord as well as the fact that all they had was a gift from Him.

THE BEGINNING OF THE PRIESTHOOD
Read Leviticus 9:7–24

What is God's response to the offerings? What is Israel's response?

_____

_____

_____

Insight

Through Leviticus 8, Moses is the prominent leader of Israel. However, beginning with the installation of the priesthood, Aaron's leadership becomes more and more visible as well. Moses' provisional priestly role seems to be coming to an end. He is the great prophet, but Aaron is the great priest.

CLEAN AND UNCLEAN FOOD
Read Leviticus 11:1–12

Why do you think God cares what sort of food His people eat?

_____

_____

_____

BEING HOLY
Read Leviticus 19:1–18

List one or two themes that run throughout these laws.

_____

_____

_____

What refrain shows up again and again? Why do you think this is?

_____

_____

_____

Critical Observation

When God gave the Israelites the Ten Commandments on Mount Sinai, He began by saying, "I am the LORD thy God, which have brought thee out of the land of Egypt, out of the house of bondage" (Exodus 20:2). When the Law of Moses was repeated to the next generation, the same phrase was spoken (Deuteronomy 5:6). In the laws of Leviticus, we frequently see the first part of this phrase, "I am the LORD," stated to the people. It is repeated more than forty times in Leviticus 18–26 alone. These words reminded the Israelites of their identity as the people of God, having been rescued by Him from slavery in Egypt.

What principles about loving God and loving others appear in the laws you've read from Leviticus?

_____

_____

_____

Take It Home

For many, the Old Testament law is a long, confusing, and hopelessly outdated portion of scripture that has no real application or use for the church today. That perspective overlooks the purpose the law served for Israel. God designed the law to separate His people from the surrounding pagan nations, so that they might better serve Him. Are you set apart for God's work? Does your life look any different now that you know Christ? Are there any reminders in your life that point you back to the Lord?

Connecting the Story Line

- The law showed Israel their sin and need for a solution, ultimately in a savior. Jesus Christ provided the path to salvation we need.

- The law provides a number of images to help us better understand Jesus. The New Testament speaks of His death as a sacrifice (Hebrews 10). Elsewhere He is called the high priest who will forever intercede for His people (Hebrews 9:11).

Day 12
Joshua and Jericho

Setting Up the Story
Joshua succeeds Moses as the leader of God's people. He leads the people into the Promised Land through miraculous military victories and unlikely battle strategies. His leadership begins when he sends spies into Jericho to gather information on the city. The spies stay at the house of a woman named Rahab, who hides them from the king of Jericho. When the Israelites conquer Jericho, Rahab is rewarded for her faith and allowed to join Israel, even though she is a Gentile.

If you have time, read the whole story: Joshua 5:13–6:27

The Plan for Victory
Read Joshua 6:1–7
When you first read this story, what was your reaction to God's plan for the Israelites to conquer Jericho? If you were Joshua, what would you have thought after hearing that plan?

_____

_____

_____

Insight
The directions given to Joshua by God for the conquest of Jericho seem strange, but not if we think in biblical terms about the life of faith and humanity's inherent inability to accomplish God's plans on our own. Victory is always by the Lord's hand, and it is unsurprising for God to work in ways that only He can.

Why is it significant that the priests and the ark of the covenant led the procession around Jericho?

Critical Observation

The number seven is used eleven times in chapter 6. Seven signifies perfection or completion, which reminds us that God's plan is always perfect and cannot be improved upon (Romans 11:33–36; 12:2; 1 Corinthians 1:18). Further, the number seven shows that the conquest is part of a spiritual exercise designed to set the people apart (sanctify them) for the Lord as a holy people who belong to a holy God. Because of the significance of the number seven to creation and the Sabbath, and the fact they were entering into their inheritance, it also signifies the beginning of a new order and the land as a picture of the believer's rest in the Lord (Hebrews 4).

THE PATH TO VICTORY

Read Joshua 6:8–21

How do you think seeing the walls of Jericho fall strengthened the Israelites' faith in God and His promises?

Insight

Joshua did not reveal the entire plan to Israel at once, but day by day he gave them instructions to go out and march around the city. It took faith for the people to obey, faith that was rewarded on the seventh day when the walls of the city fell by the hand of God.

THE PROMISE FULFILLED
Read Joshua 6:22–27
What is surprising about the woman who is spared?

_____

_____

_____

What do these verses reveal about God's attributes and character traits?

_____

_____

_____

In what ways do you suspect that the events of Joshua 6:27 will impact Joshua's future battles?

_____

_____

_____

Take It Home
The people marched silently around Jericho despite the taunts that were likely hurled at them from the residents of the city. They were willing to look foolish for the Lord, who was their source of strength. If we want to overcome our obstacles, we must also submit to God's way by faith (Galatians 5:5).

Joshua's story also reminds us that the Lord can work slowly. We want immediate deliverance, but the Lord often tests our faith and in the process builds our character and relationship with Him so that we find the Lord to be what we really need (James 1:2–4).

Connecting the Story Line

- God shows that He will do miracles for the protection of His people.

- God continues to deliver on His promise to Abraham by preserving His people and giving them the land.

- The story of Rahab demonstrates God's grace to all people. Even more, she becomes an ancestor of Christ (see Matthew 1:5).

DAY 13
SAUL

SETTING UP THE STORY

After Joshua helps settle the people in the land, the people of Israel live as a loose confederation of tribes. These tribes are united and led by occasional leaders (called judges) who free them from the oppression of various raiding parties and enemies. After a number of generations, the people want to organize around a king like the other nations they know. Though a prophet named Samuel warns them of specific dangers a monarchy would bring, the people are persistent in their desire for a king.

If you have time, read the whole story:
1 Samuel 8:1–11:13; 13; 14:15–15:35

A KING IS ANOINTED
Read 1 Samuel 9:15–10:1
How do the circumstances of Saul and Samuel's meeting demonstrate God's sovereignty?

_____

_____

_____

SAUL'S MILITARY SUCCESS
Read 1 Samuel 11:1–13
What does Saul's military success do for him and for Israel?

_____

_____

_____

Insight

Most of what has been written about Saul so far has been positive. He has displayed strong leadership, physical strength, and military skill. As a result, he has the full support of the people. However, things soon begin to go badly for Saul as he fails to trust in God and obey Him.

SAUL DISOBEYS THE LORD
Read 1 Samuel 13:8–14
What is wrong with Saul's actions? What do they say about his trust in God?

_____

_____

_____

Critical Observation

Perhaps Saul believed that the offering itself would be the means for Israel's deliverance, in much the same way that the Israelites believed that taking the ark into battle would ensure God's blessing (1 Samuel 4:3–11). If so, it is no wonder that Saul is so determined to offer the sacrifice— with or without Samuel.

Note that Samuel appears just as Saul makes the offering, in plenty of time to have made the offering himself. Saul is unable to rebuke Samuel for being late. Rather, it is Samuel who demands an explanation from Saul.

MORE BAD DECISIONS
Read 1 Samuel 14:24–35
What do you think motivates Saul's oath? What does this demonstrate about his faith?

_____

_____

_____

How does Jonathan's character contrast with Saul's?

_____
_____
_____

Insight

Saul had been long intimidated, if not humiliated, by the Philistines, and he is determined to make them pay. Therefore, he places his soldiers under oath and forbids them to eat until evening, most likely to not waste time stopping for a meal. However, this oath betrays a lack of trust in God and His ability to provide.

THE LORD WITHDRAWS FROM SAUL
Read 1 Samuel 15:10–29
List several reasons God takes the kingdom away from Saul.

_____
_____
_____

Take It Home

It may seem from a casual reading that Saul made one mistake and lost his kingdom as a result, which could make God appear vindictive or petty. In all likelihood, the examples the Bible records are representative of many events from Saul's life. It was his duty as king to know God's laws and carefully observe them (see Deuteronomy 17:18–20). He ignores those general commands, as well as the specific instructions of the Lord's prophet, Samuel (1 Samuel 10:8). Like Saul, if we have no sense of our calling, we are headed for trouble. The emergencies of life are not excuses to disobey God's commands; they test our faith and obedience. God often works through less than perfect people like Saul—and like us. If we can learn from

Saul's mistakes and trust God more, we can become much more effective in our individual ministries.

Connecting the Story Line

• Saul's disobedience demonstrates the inherent human tendency to disobey and distrust God, despite His love for us. What we need is faith obtained through God's grace.

• Saul's failures pave the way for David's kingship. When the people had demanded a king, God gave them the kind of king they were looking for. In contrast, David becomes the kind of king God wants for His people. David will rule all Israel for forty years and become an ancestor of Christ.

Day 14
Samuel and David

Setting Up the Story
In the last reading, we saw that Samuel walked away from Saul and never visited him again (1 Samuel 15:35).

It isn't long, though, until God sends Samuel on an assignment to anoint Saul's replacement as king of Israel. Samuel is not told in advance who this person will be and must trust God to show him the way.

If you have time, read the whole story: 1 Samuel 16:1–23

Samuel's Journey to Bethlehem
Read 1 Samuel 16:1–5
Why does Samuel travel to Bethlehem despite the danger from Saul?

_____

_____

_____

Insight
Samuel had already told Saul that he was going to lose his kingship. As a result, Saul became paranoid and suspicious, particularly of David. After David's early military success, Saul regarded him with increasing jealousy.

Why do you think God does not immediately tell Samuel who the next king will be?

_____

_____

_____

Critical Observation

When Samuel received the Lord's instructions to go to Bethlehem and anoint a new king, he feared that Saul would kill him. After all, Saul had just annihilated nearly all of the Amalekites, and he also showed himself willing to put his own son to death (1 Samuel 14:44). To make matters worse, Samuel would have to travel through Saul's hometown of Gibeah to go from Ramah to Bethlehem. Though Saul might not know exactly what Samuel's instructions were, he would likely suspect that Samuel was searching for a new king, since he had previously rejected Saul's kingship. Given these dangers, it would take faith for Samuel to continue on his journey.

SAMUEL LOOKS AT THE OUTSIDE
Read 1 Samuel 16:6–10
What do you think it means to look at the heart of someone?

_____

_____

_____

SAMUEL ANOINTS DAVID
Read 1 Samuel 16:11–13
What is significant about David, the youngest brother, being chosen as king? What does this tell us about God?

_____

_____

_____

In what other biblical stories have you already seen God's work through the younger brother? (If you need a reminder, see the Critical Observation in Day 6.)

_____

_____

_____

Insight

Samuel assumed the oldest and strongest brother would be anointed king, but God had other plans. If David's heart was right, God would provide everything else Israel's king needed. When Samuel anoints David in the presence of his other family members, God's Spirit falls powerfully on him.

Read 1 Samuel 16:14–23

David is selected to serve in Saul's court. In what ways might his proximity to the king prepare him for his own future reign?

_____

_____

_____

Take It Home

Consider again the words of God in 1 Samuel 16:7, which remind us that God looks at the hearts of people, not their outward appearances. God does not show favoritism toward those who are the strongest, best looking, or most talented. He judges by a person's character and spiritual well-being. Samuel thought that David's older and stronger brothers would be good kings, but God had other plans. When do you judge others by outward appearances? Are you guilty of showing partiality to those who look the best? Or conversely, do you ever feel judged or ignored because you are not the most talented or best looking? Take heart. God loves you and sees you truly for who you are: His child.

Connecting the Story Line

- Throughout Hebrew history, David is remembered as the ideal king. Even the Jews of Jesus' day were longing for a king from the line of David to restore glory and power to Israel. Though Jesus would become that king, His kingdom was not what the people expected.

- David became a direct ancestor of Jesus, who would often be referred to as the "son of David" (Matthew 9:27).

Day 15
David and Goliath

Setting Up the Story
Though God has rejected Saul's kingship and David has secretly been anointed the next king of Israel, Saul still reigns over the people. The Philistines, the primary enemy of the people, have gathered to wage war against Israel. The armies of both countries camp across from each other and prepare for battle. Every day at the front lines, a giant soldier named Goliath mocks and challenges the Israelites, but no one can stop him. To Israel it seems impossible to defeat Goliath and the Philistines, but because David trusts God, he has a different perspective.

If you have time, read the whole story: 1 Samuel 17

Israel Intimidated
Read 1 Samuel 17:8–11
What do you imagine the Israelites are thinking as they see Goliath every day?

_____

_____

_____

David Seeks to Defend Israel
Read 1 Samuel 17:25–30
Why do you think David's brother Eliab reacts to David this way?

_____

_____

_____

Insight

David is acting like the king of Israel should act. He trusts God, takes action to defeat the Lord's enemies, and inspires his fellow Israelites to do the same. Saul gives David every opportunity, first to excuse himself and go home, and then to arm himself before fighting. But David has a confidence based in faith. He trusts God to provide him the victory.

DAVID EXPLAINS HIMSELF TO SAUL

Read 1 Samuel 17:31–37

What metaphor does David use for himself and Goliath, and how is it effective?

_____

_____

_____

Critical Observation

Note what a contrast is made when David is introduced to the story. Goliath is described in physical terms of appearance, weaponry, and aggressiveness. But nothing is said of David's stature, strength, or weapons. Rather, he is introduced in the context of his family. One reason has already been mentioned: David was chosen because of his heart, not his outer physical qualities (1 Samuel 13:14; 16:7). Another reason is that the Messiah will come from the tribe of Judah and from Bethlehem (Genesis 49:8–12; Micah 5:2). Jesus will eventually trace His human ancestry back to David.

DAVID REFUSES SAUL'S ARMOR

Read 1 Samuel 17:38–44

Why is it significant that David doesn't wear armor to fight Goliath?

_____

_____

_____

DAVID KILLS GOLIATH
Read 1 Samuel 17:45–52

Most people assume the story of David and Goliath ends with the well-placed shot from David's sling. What does 1 Samuel 17:51 reveal about David's final move against the giant?

_____

_____

_____

Insight

Though Goliath was armored head to foot and protected by both shield and armor-bearer, he still needed an opening around his eyes to see. David used his accuracy with a sling to send the first stone into Goliath's exposed forehead.

What does David's defeat of Goliath accomplish for the Israelites?

_____

_____

_____

Take It Home

The account of David and Goliath is a good reminder of how God promises to care for and protect His faithful people. When Saul's fear became evident, Israel's soldiers were also frightened (1 Samuel 17:11), but after David stood up to Goliath, the other troops became courageous. It shouldn't matter how large our obstacles are. If we remain in a proper relationship with the Lord, He will continue to protect us and provide for us. And as we grow in this faith, others will be comforted alongside us.

Connecting the Story Line

- David's heroics help spread his fame across Israel and pave the way for his coming kingship. He is already acting and leading as a king would.

- The story demonstrates David's faith in God, which he will need during his upcoming forty-year reign. This same faith is also evident in many of the psalms that he writes. (You can read much about David's reign in the book of 2 Samuel.)

DAY 16
SOLOMON

SETTING UP THE STORY
We now fast-forward over forty years since yesterday's reading. First Kings begins dramatically in the twilight of David's glorious reign over Israel, as the question of David's successor remains unresolved. His oldest son, Adonijah, has his eyes on the throne and attempts to claim it without David's permission. The next king of Israel, however, will not be determined by the rules of hereditary succession, as God has other plans. After Bathsheba, David's wife, learns of Adonijah's plan, she and Nathan, a prophet of God, work to establish Solomon as king.

If you have time, read the whole story: 1 Kings 1–11

SOLOMON MADE KING
Read 1 Kings 1:28–40
How would you contrast Solomon's ascent to the throne with Adonijah's attempt to take it?

_____

_____

_____

SOLOMON ASKS FOR WISDOM
Read 1 Kings 3:5–15
Why does God reward Solomon's request for wisdom?

_____

_____

_____

Insight

Under Solomon's rule, Israel was a large and prosperous state. Solomon himself becomes a prominent and famous man, using his wisdom to solve problems and write songs and proverbs (1 Kings 4:32). Many of Solomon's wise sayings are found in the biblical book of Proverbs.

SOLOMON BUILDS THE TEMPLE
Read 1 Kings 6:11–38

What does God promise Solomon regarding Himself and the temple?

_____

_____

_____

Critical Observation

Though the temple was beautiful, it was not for the people of Israel; it was only for the priests to meet with God on behalf of the people. The people gathered and worshipped in the outer courtyard.

Insight

Solomon spent seven years building the temple but almost twice as long (thirteen years) building his palace. While the temple was a glorious structure, the text suggests that perhaps Solomon wanted his palace to be even more magnificent. This may be a first indication that Solomon was beginning to wander from the God-centered priorities that once marked his reign.

THE BEGINNING OF SOLOMON'S DECLINE
Read 1 Kings 11:1–13

List some of the things that cause Solomon to stumble in his faith.

_____

_____

_____

Critical Observation

Marrying a foreign woman was not against the Law of Moses, as long as she became a convert to the God of Israel. Ruth, for example, was a Moabitess who returned to Bethlehem with her mother-in-law, Naomi, and adopted Naomi's faith, eventually marrying into Naomi's family. This practice was not the case, however, with Solomon. First Kings tells us that Solomon amassed a thousand foreign wives and concubines, who shipwrecked his faith in the Lord by turning him toward false gods and idols.

How does God respond to Solomon's actions? Why do you suppose God acts this way?

_____

_____

_____

Take It Home

Solomon was perhaps the wisest man who ever lived. The proverbs he wrote are still read and recognized for their wisdom today. He also ruled over a massive kingdom and possessed unfathomable wealth and fame. Yet even he was drawn away from the Lord, the source of his prosperity, and prone to stray and worship other gods. If Solomon could fail, we must never think that we are too smart or too pious to be above failure ourselves. Only through dependence on Jesus Christ and His mercy and faithfulness can we live godly lives.

Connecting the Story Line

- Solomon continues the kingship of the line of David, the fulfillment of God's promise that David will always have an heir to his throne. This is ultimately fulfilled in the reign of Christ.

- The temple built by Solomon represents God's presence among His people. It would be destroyed when Judah was defeated and taken into exile, then rebuilt and destroyed again after the time of Jesus. Controversy surrounding the temple continues to this day.

- Solomon's decline brings the first mention that the kingdom of Israel will be divided. This division, into northern and southern kingdoms, would become a reality for hundreds of years afterward.

DAY 17
THE DIVISION OF THE KINGDOM

SETTING UP THE STORY
Near the end of Solomon's reign, God reveals the
consequences that result from his defiance of the Lord's
decrees (1 Kings 11:11–12). As a result of his sin, the
kingdom of Israel will be shattered and taken from his
heirs. Only the tribes of Judah and Benjamin will remain,
in honor of God's promise to David. The man whom
God raises up to lead the remaining tribes is Jeroboam.
He rebels against Solomon and opposes Rehoboam,
Solomon's heir. Though appointed by God, Jeroboam
quickly leads the people into evil behavior.

If you have time, read the whole story: 1 Kings 11:14–14:31

JEROBOAM REBELS AGAINST SOLOMON
Read 1 Kings 11:26–40
Why is it surprising that God would raise up another king?

_____

_____

_____

Insight
God promises a lasting dynasty for Jeroboam if he will do
what is right in the Lord's eyes. In many ways, Jeroboam
begins his rule in a situation similar to that of Israel's great
king, David. Both Jeroboam and David are appointed by the
Lord, and both are given the opportunity to receive God's
blessing and a long-lasting dynasty. However, while David
trusted the Lord and waited patiently for His guidance,
Jeroboam refused to wait on God and often worshipped
idols.

REHOBOAM MISTREATS ISRAEL
Read 1 Kings 12:1–16
What is Rehoboam's fundamental mistake?

_____

_____

_____

THE REBELLION GETS VIOLENT
Read 1 Kings 12:18–24
Why do you suppose that God does not want Israel and Judah to fight?

_____

_____

_____

JEROBOAM PRACTICES APOSTASY
Read 1 Kings 12:25–33
What is Jeroboam's motivation for his actions? In what way is it misguided?

_____

_____

_____

Critical Observation
Jeroboam repeats similar mistakes of Aaron, who, five hundred years before, had presented a golden calf to the people and said: "These are your gods, O Israel" (Exodus 32:4 NIV). It is bad enough for Jeroboam to disobey God, but even worse for him to lead others into disobedience as well. He continues to build additional places of worship outside the main worship centers at Bethel and Dan and creates his own religious holidays. He also goes so far as to establish his own priesthood, rejecting the Lord's commands regarding the priesthood.

GOD'S PROPHECY AGAINST JEROBOAM
Read 1 Kings 14:1–11
What does this story reveal about Jeroboam?

_____

_____

_____

What made Jeroboam worse than the rulers who came before him?

_____

_____

_____

Take It Home
God gave Jeroboam an amazing opportunity to lead ten tribes of Israel out of sin and back to the Lord, perhaps restoring the sort of peace and prosperity that were once characteristic of David's and Solomon's reigns. He had the Lord's backing and the resources to accomplish His purposes, yet he chose to ignore God's commands. Similarly, there are times when God gives us amazing gifts and opportunities. The Lord's call on our lives is to devote everything we have, however big or small, to serve Him.

Connecting the Story Line

- The divided kingdom never unites again and is the subject and setting for the conflict found in the biblical prophetic books.

- Israel's and Judah's kings, beginning with Jeroboam, provide some of the Bible's best examples of wicked and godly behavior.

- God demonstrates His faithfulness to His promises by sustaining the kingdom of Judah, which will be ruled forever by a descendant of David: Jesus Christ.

DAY 18
THE FALL OF THE NORTHERN KINGDOM
(ISRAEL)

SETTING UP THE STORY

The kingdom of Israel has been divided for a little more than two hundred years, ever since the end of King Solomon's reign. Though both kingdoms—Israel (also known as Samaria) to the north and Judah to the south—have struggled to obey the Lord, Israel has been particularly prone to ungodly leadership and the worship of false idols. As a result, God has allowed Assyria to conquer them and lead them into exile. This doesn't happen because God is unable to protect them but because He has given them over to their sin. Unlike the southern kingdom, the people of the northern kingdom will never return from their exile.

If you have time, read the whole story: 2 Kings 17:1–41

THE FALL OF SAMARIA
Read 2 Kings 17:1–6
List the mistakes that cost Hoshea's downfall. What do you think this story has to tell us about trust?

Insight
The fall of the northern kingdom was not simply the result of Hoshea's reign. From the time the northern kingdom was established, the people had abandoned God and were led by evil kings. Despite warning after warning, the people of the northern kingdom (and their kings)

stubbornly continued down sinful paths. Eventually God had enough and allowed the Assyrians to conquer them.

Critical Observation
When the Assyrians depopulated and exiled a conquered community, they lead the captives away on a journey of hundreds of miles. Often the captives were naked and attached to one another by a system of strings and fishhooks through their lower lips. The experience would have been both painful and incredibly humiliating. Whether the Israelites realized it was a result of their sin or not, they may have felt like the Lord had abandoned them.

THE REASONS FOR THE FALL
Read 2 Kings 17:7–15
How would you summarize the reasons for Israel's exile?

_____

_____

_____

Insight
The exile marked the end of the ten northern tribes as an independent kingdom. After they were dispersed by the Assyrians, some assimilated into other cultures, while others maintained their Jewish identity in exile.

THE RESETTLEMENT OF SAMARIA
Read 2 Kings 17:24–33
What are the results of the resettlement?

_____

_____

_____

What do the foreign settlers wrongly assume about the Lord?

_____

_____

_____

Insight

The policy of the Assyrian Empire is to remove rebellious and resistant people and resettle their former lands with residents from other parts of the empire. These newcomers do not fear God, so He sends lions among then. This demonstrates not only that there is something special about the kingdom of Israel but also that there is something special about the land of Israel. Ironically, the Assyrian officials realize more quickly than Israel ever did that God demands honor, though they fail to realize that the Lord demands to be worshipped alone as God.

What does the exile of the northern kingdom reveal about God?

_____

_____

_____

Take It Home

Israel had failed as a kingdom. The citizens and their kings lived disobedient lives, ignored God's law and will, and as a result suffered a humiliating defeat and exile. They must have been left in great pain and confusion. We also will fail in life, sometimes as a result of our own weaknesses and shortcomings, and sometimes for reasons out of our control. The question to ask in failure is, How will I respond? Consider a past or present failure in your own life. What can you learn from it that will strengthen your faith today?

Connecting the Story Line

- The exile of the northern kingdom (and later the southern kingdom as well) reminds readers that God takes sin very seriously. While complacency is common, God expects His people to persevere in their faith.

- As a result of the people's sin, the northern kingdom of Israel is removed from the land promised to Abraham hundreds of years before. Not all is lost, however. Judah remains faithful to God, and even after the people of Judah experience their own exile, God will bring back some them to repopulate the land and rebuild the temple. (You can read about these events in the books of Ezra and Nehemiah.)

DAY 19
THE FALL OF THE SOUTHERN KINGDOM
(JUDAH)

SETTING UP THE STORY

The northern kingdom had already fallen, and now the southern kingdom was in peril. Only a few generations before, King Josiah of Judah had rediscovered the book of the Law and renewed Israel's covenant with the Lord. However, since then Judah had lived under ungodly and faithless leadership, which had exacerbated their problems and contributed to their ultimate exile at the hands of the Babylonians. As chapter 24 ends and 25 begins, King Nebuchadnezzar of Babylon has already visited Jerusalem, removed the king, and installed a puppet government led by King Zedekiah. When Zedekiah foolishly rebels, Nebuchadnezzar returns to finish what he started.

If you have time, read the whole story: 2 Kings 24:18–25:30

ZEDEKIAH REBELS
Read 2 Kings 24:18–20
Why does God allow the exile of the southern kingdom?

_____

_____

_____

Insight
Both the prophets Jeremiah and Ezekiel prophesied against King Zedekiah. Ezekiel offered some specific words about his fate in Ezekiel 12:13, words that would be fulfilled by his capture and exile at the hands of Nebuchadnezzar.

NEBUCHADNEZZAR CAPTURES JERUSALEM
Read 2 Kings 25:1–10

List the events that occur during Zedekiah's devastating defeat.

_____

_____

_____

Critical Observation
When Nebuchadnezzar attacks Jerusalem, he uses the method common in those days against securely walled cities, a siege. During a siege, the city would be surrounded and no business or trade would go in or out. The city would slowly starve until it decided to surrender. The siege in Jerusalem lasts a year and a half, at which point the famine is so severe that Zedekiah and the people reach a point of desperation. They make a last-ditch effort to escape and break through the Babylonian siege lines, acting not in faith but in fear (2 Kings 25:4). For a moment, it might look like the plan works, but Nebuchadnezzar's army is too strong and fast, and Judah cannot escape the Lord's judgment.

THE JEWS ARE CARRIED INTO EXILE
Read 2 Kings 25:11–12

What benefits do you suppose Nebuchadnezzar hopes to gain with this strategy?

_____

_____

_____

THE TEMPLE IS SACKED
Read 2 Kings 25:13–21

What do you think the destruction of the temple symbolizes to the people of the southern kingdom?

_____

_____

_____

If you were alive during this time and watching these events, what do you think you'd be feeling as they unfolded?

_____

_____

_____

Insight
This situation greatly bothers the prophet Habakkuk. Even though Judah is wicked and deserves judgment, how can God use an equally wicked kingdom like Babylon to bring about His judgment? Habakkuk wrestles with these difficult questions in Habakkuk 1:5–2:8.

NEBUCHADNEZZAR'S MIGHTY HAND
Read 2 Kings 25:22–30

What do these verses reveal about the strength of Nebuchadnezzar's reign?

_____

_____

_____

Take It Home
The siege of Jerusalem and subsequent capture at the hands of the Babylonians would have been a terrifying ordeal for the citizens of Judah. After facing a year and a half of potential starvation, Zedekiah and his army were pursued for miles and overtaken on the plains of Jericho.

Their attempt to break through the siege lines had been an act of desperation. When all hope seemed lost, Judah had responded not in faith but in fear. Fittingly, it was this same lack of faith that had contributed to the sinful behavior that led to the exile in the first place. What is your response to a difficult situation you are currently facing?

Connecting the Story Line

- The Jewish people are removed from the land promised to Abraham and his descendants hundreds of years before. Though God had delivered the land to them through a number of miraculous events, the people had became enamored with other gods and caught up in their own wickedness.

- The story of the people of God is not over. The stories of Esther and Daniel still lay ahead, and eventually a small, more humble remnant will return to the Promised Land. Under the leadership of Ezra, Nehemiah, and Zerubbabel, the people will eventually rebuild the temple and city walls. They will live in the land until they are conquered by the Romans just before Israel's long-awaited Messiah, Jesus Christ, arrives.

DAY 20
ESTHER

SETTING UP THE STORY
Due to their continued disobedience and pursuit of idolatry, God allows the people of the northern and southern kingdoms to be conquered and exiled, by the Assyrians and Babylonians, respectively. In turn, the Persians conquer the Babylonians, so that the Jewish people now live under Persian rule. During this time of captivity, Esther rises to prominence in the Persian court and faces a challenge that will threaten the existence of her people.

If you have time, read the whole story: Esther 1–10

ESTHER BECOMES QUEEN
Read Esther 2:8–18
How do you think Esther feels, living in the king's court while hiding her Jewish heritage?

_____

_____

_____

HAMAN PLOTS TO KILL THE JEWS
Read Esther 3:1–11
What motivates Haman's actions? Why?

_____

_____

_____

Critical Observation
One of the few things we are told about Haman is that he is an Agagite, and thus a descendant of the Amalekites. Mordecai, by contrast, is a Benjamite—the tribe of King

Saul. Israelites and Amalekites had long been bitter enemies. Before Israel even crossed from Egypt to Canaan, they were fighting the Amalekites, and God promised Moses their eventual destruction (Deuteronomy 25:17–19). Later, King Saul was instructed to kill King Agag of the Amalekites (1 Samuel 15).

Understanding this history sheds additional light on the conflict between Mordecai and Haman. Not only is Haman offended that Mordecai will not bow down to him, but he also might harbor anger and distrust toward the Jewish people in general. Thus he doesn't want to stop at killing Mordecai; he wants to kill all of the Jews.

MORDECAI PERSUADES ESTHER TO HELP
Read Esther 4:11–17
What challenge does Esther face? How does she respond?

_____

_____

_____

Insight
The New International Version of the Bible translates Mordecai's remark to Esther, "And who knows but that you have come to royal position for such a time as this?" (4:14). Mordecai is willing to see God's providential hand at work, even in difficult circumstances. He believes God has led Esther to this point so that she might save the Jews.

ESTHER REVEALS HAMAN'S PLOT
Read Esther 7:1–10
What is the great irony in this section of the story?

_____

_____

_____

MORDECAI AND ESTHER ARE HONORED
Read Esther 8:1–2, 15–17

God is never directly mentioned in the book of Esther. In what ways, though, do you see God at work behind the scenes in this story?

Insight

Not only does Esther receive everything Haman owned, but Mordecai also takes his place of honor in the court. We see a complete reversal from Haman's plan to God's plan, as Haman is hanged on the gallows meant for Mordecai, and Mordecai instead assumes Haman's position among the royal officials.

Take It Home

God's actions and direction are evident throughout the story of Esther. This story illustrates a wonderful point—that God is always at work in the circumstances of our lives, whether we can see it or not. He will never abandon us. It can be difficult to trust God when He seems absent, but the scriptures proclaim God's steadfast faithfulness and love. We can rely on Him. Do you struggle to trust God when He seems distant? What are instances from your own life where you can see God's hand at work, even if it wasn't apparent at the time?

Connecting the Story Line

- The Jews faced extinction because of Haman's plot, but God used Mordecai and Esther to preserve His people.

- God has been continually faithful to His people throughout the Old Testament, even when they were not in possession of the Promised Land. God is most concerned with His relationship with His people. His primary concern is not a specific geographic land.

Day 21
Job

Setting Up the Story

The book of Job has been called a masterpiece unequaled in all literature. Job is a man, "perfect and upright" (Job 1:1), whom the Lord allows to suffer at the hands of Satan. The book of Job contains a powerful, in-depth discussion on the nature of suffering, man's response to it, and humanity's relationship to God. Job's friends presumptuously accuse him of sin, yet God's response reveals that His ways are higher than ours, often beyond comprehension—and that suffering is not always a result of wrongdoing.

If you have time, read the whole story: Job 1–42

Job Is Tested
Read Job 1:6–22; 2:3–10
Does it surprise you that God would allow this to happen? Why or why not?

_____

_____

_____

Critical Observation
Though the book of Job appears in the middle of the Bible, the books of the Bible are not always arranged chronologically. Job is likely a contemporary of Abraham. Scholars conclude this for several reasons: First, Job's long life (140 years after his suffering) is consistent with the life spans of men of that time. Second, despite Job's worship of the Lord, there is no mention anywhere of the Mosaic Law. And third, Job's wealth is described in terms of livestock, not money, which is consistent with the rich men who lived during Abraham's time.

JOB SPEAKS
Read Job 3:11–19
Do you believe Job is right or wrong to feel this way?

_____

_____

_____

HIS FRIENDS ACCUSE HIM
Read Job 4:7–21
What incorrect assumption do Job's friends have?

_____

_____

Insight
Job is in so much pain and misery that he wishes he had never been born. Though Job is often characterized as being patient in suffering, it is more accurate to say that he was perseverant. Job feels his pain as much as anyone would, yet he refuses to accuse God of wrongdoing.

Job's friend Eliphaz concludes that Job is suffering because of his sin—he thinks that only the wicked endure trials like these. This simplistic approach is not a scriptural truth. The Bible has many examples of the righteous suffering, none greater than Jesus on the cross.

JOB RESPONDS TO HIS FRIENDS
Read Job 31:1–12
How does Job respond to his friends?

_____

_____

_____

GOD SPEAKS
Read Job 38:1–7; 40:1–5
Summarize God's overall exchange with Job.

_____

_____

_____

Insight
Job has a different perspective of God at the end of the book. First of all, Job recognizes the sovereignty of God and that He is in control of everything (42:1–2). God shows Job that He not only created the heavens and the earth and all that dwell in them, but He sustains them also. Everything is subject to His sovereign rule.

Second, Job recognizes the foolishness of his words. Job has spoken about issues he knew nothing about (42:3), and yet he sounded so sure of himself. God redirects Job to fall back on the things he knows about God instead of coming up with foolish conclusions about life's situations.

It is one thing to hear God but quite another thing to encounter God (42:4–5). It is Job's encounter with God that causes him to see himself as a sinner, and he repents of his sin (42:6).

JOB IS RESTORED
Read Job 42:12–17
What surprising twist does the end of Job's story take?

_____

_____

_____

Take It Home

It is easy to see the world in simple cause-and-effect terms. It is also tempting to think that we understand everything perfectly after a surface-level glance. The book of Job is a call to humility, not only in the face of our own suffering, but also when facing the suffering of others. God is a loving and merciful God, but He is also holy and mighty and beyond our comprehension. We should not presume that we will always understand everything about Him or the events of our lives.

Connecting the Story Line

- The story of Job does not intersect directly with other Bible stories, but it does teach us about God and human suffering.

- Job reminds us of the reality of both God and Satan and their cosmic conflict with each other. It is this adversarial relationship that we first see in the Fall (Genesis 3), and it will continue to exist until the arrival of the new heaven and new earth described in the book of Revelation.

- Throughout history, and in both the Old and New Testaments, the people of God have suffered for a variety of reasons, including their faith in the Lord. The book of Job is a real confrontation with pain and suffering, and it has been a comfort for many as they seek to understand their own circumstances.

DAY 22
THE PSALMS

SETTING UP THE STORY

The Psalms were written by a variety of authors throughout Old Testament history. They demonstrate the witness of godly people confronting themselves, their circumstances, and the Lord with honesty and reverence. Many psalms offer praise to God, but there are also psalms that lament wickedness and cry out for God's presence when He seems distant. The Psalms deepen our understanding of God and what it means to live as His servants in the world.

If you have time, read the whole story: Psalms 1–150

THE LORD IS MY SHEPHERD
Read Psalm 23

What are some of the images the psalmist uses? How do they help you understand his point?

_____

_____

_____

Critical Observation

The psalmists frequently employ poetic imagery to communicate their point. Psalm 23 is a good example. David uses the picture of God as a shepherd to illustrate the people's relationship with Him. While the rod is typically viewed as a punishing tool, it was also often used for gentle correction. A shepherd could nudge a wayward sheep and prevent it from straying off the safe path. Thus when David writes, "thy rod and thy staff they comfort me" (23:4), he is painting a picture of God's protection and care.

A CRY FOR MERCY
Read Psalm 51
How does an understanding of the psalm's context with David and Bathsheba inform your reading? (Read that story in 2 Samuel 11.)

_____

_____

_____

A PSALM OF LAMENT
Read Psalm 74
What seems to motivate the writing of this psalm?

_____

_____

_____

Insight
Several psalms, including Psalm 74, were likely written after the people had been conquered and exiled to Babylon (see Day 19). The loss of the temple and the beloved city of Jerusalem was difficult for many Jews. While they recognized that it was the result of their own sin, they still struggled to know God in their new surroundings.

SHOUT FOR JOY
Read Psalm 100
List some reasons the psalmist gives for worshipping the Lord.

_____

_____

_____

A CALL FOR RESCUE

Read Psalm 140

Describe a modern situation or example that would capture the feelings of the psalmist.

_____

_____

_____

Insight

Though many psalms offer honest laments and questions for God, they still usually end with an affirmation of trust in the Lord. Despite their difficult circumstances, the psalm writers affirm that God is sovereign and faithful.

Read Psalm 148

How could you put this psalm into your own words?

_____

_____

_____

Take It Home

The psalms portray an honest and open relationship with God. They do not deny the struggles and pain in life, but they nonetheless continually affirm His grace and power at work in the world. Our challenge is to strive for the sometimes raw and honest faith that the psalmists had—all while maintaining their same spirit of praise and reverence. What changes to your devotional or prayer life would help you develop a similar relationship with Him?

Connecting the Story Line

- The Psalms give us a great deal of personal insight into some of the Bible's most important periods, including the life of King David and the struggles of Israel and Judah in exile.

- Jesus, His disciples, and the early church used the Psalms to help communicate truth and better understand their own circumstances. Several psalms are viewed as prophecies that point to the incarnate Christ.

DAY 23
ISAIAH AND GOD'S BIG IDEAS

SETTING UP THE STORY
It is helpful to remember that the books of the Bible are not always in chronological order. The book of Isaiah was written around the time of Israel's fall to Assyria (see Day 18), and only a little more than a century before Judah's fall to Babylon (see Day 19). Israel and Judah are caught in the middle of a giant political struggle between Assyria, Egypt, and Babylon. They have struggled and often failed to keep their own identities as people of God, offering loyalty to one or more foreign nations instead of to the Lord. Isaiah's masterful work is far-reaching in its scope and offers guidance, judgment, and hope to Israel and the nations surrounding it. It provides different pictures of the future realities of judgment and restoration for Israel and the world.

If you have time, read the whole story:
Isaiah 1–13; 53–55; 65–66

JUDGMENT AND HOPE FOR ISRAEL
Read Isaiah 1:21–28
Why do you think God equates the spiritual straying of the people with prostitution (see 1:21)?

_____

_____

_____

PROPHECIES AGAINST THE NATIONS
Read Isaiah 13:1–13
What is God's message for Babylon?

_____

_____

_____

Critical Observation

Though portions of biblical prophecy deal with future events, the prophets were more often concerned with speaking the word of the Lord to the people of their day, whether kings of Israel and Judah, foreign governments, or the Jewish people in general. Isaiah contains a number of warnings directed at other nations that existed during the time, including Babylon, Assyria, Moab, and Egypt. Though God used Babylon and Assyria as instruments of judgment on Israel and Judah, He warned them that they were not exempt from their own judgment. All nations will be held accountable for their actions.

THE SUFFERING SERVANT

Read Isaiah 53:1–6

This passage is considered a prophecy about Jesus Christ. What insight does it offer about Him?

_____

_____

_____

Insight

Throughout the last portion of the book, Isaiah speaks of a Servant of the Lord who will lead the people and whose coming will make things right in the world. However, Isaiah 53 shows us that this Servant will also suffer because of other people's sins. Jesus' life, death, and resurrection were the perfect fulfillment of this prophecy.

NEW HEAVENS AND NEW EARTH
Read Isaiah 65:17–25

Based on this passage, describe the new heavens and new earth God plans to create. What will those who will live there look forward to?

_____

_____

_____

In what ways do these verses compare to the picture of the new heaven and new earth found in Revelation 21:1–5?

_____

_____

_____

Insight
Isaiah imagines a future time in which God will create new heavens and a new earth. It will be a place of joy and peace, without pain, suffering, or death, where people and God will enjoy perfect fellowship.

A FINAL PEACE
Read Isaiah 66:12–14

Toward the end of his work, Isaiah gives a great message of encouragement to the people. What do you learn about God from these verses?

_____

_____

_____

Take It Home

Many of the prophets, including Isaiah, write with a mixture of judgment and hope, a godly perspective that Christians should strive to share. We must recognize the problems and the wickedness prevalent in our world today. God takes sin very seriously, and there will be a time of judgment for all. However, because Jesus Christ bore that judgment for us, we can rest assured in God's love and promise of future restoration. Though the world is broken, God is making things right and will live in perfect fellowship with us when Christ returns again. We can begin to experience that fellowship now through Jesus and the Holy Spirit. Do you struggle to balance this perspective? Can you take sin seriously without losing hope in God's redemption?

Connecting the Story Line

- Isaiah demonstrates that there is a coming judgment for the people and nations that do not follow God.

- Isaiah provides some of the most powerful and resonant pictures by which we understand Christ's life and death.

- Isaiah gives us a glimpse of the "new heaven" that God has planned for those who follow Him. This theme is picked up elsewhere in the Bible, especially in Revelation.

DAY 24
DANIEL IN EXILE

SETTING UP THE STORY
The events that occur in the book of Daniel take place at the conclusion of the events found in 2 Kings (see Day 19). Daniel's story is told from his perspective as an exile in Babylon. As a result of persistent sin and disregard for God's laws, the Lord has allowed Judah to be conquered by Babylon, which sacks Jerusalem. Many Jews die fighting, others starve to death, and many survivors are deported to Babylon—Daniel among them. Though many of the people feel that God has deserted them, Daniel keeps faith in the Lord. He rises to prominence in the court of Nebuchadnezzar, king of Babylon, only to face several serious challenges to his loyalty to God.

If you have time, read the whole story: Daniel 1–6

NEBUCHADNEZZAR'S CHALLENGE
Read Daniel 2:1–13
What unreasonable request does Nebuchadnezzar make?

_____

_____

_____

DANIEL LEARNS OF THE CHALLENGE
Read Daniel 2:14–23
What is Daniel's response when he hears Nebuchadnezzar's news?

_____

_____

_____

Critical Observation

It was Babylonian custom for a king to relate his dreams to select advisers (sometimes called "wise men") and have them interpret the dreams for him. Nebuchadnezzar, however, took it a step further. He wanted the wise men to know his dream and interpret it without being told what it was. He had been deeply troubled by the dream and likely recognized it as divine sign. He wanted to trust the interpretation being offered to him, and he was wise enough to realize that he could not trust the astrologers and magicians. However, their astonishment at his request is understandable (Daniel 2:10). It took a miracle from God to reveal the dream.

DANIEL'S RESPONSE
Read Daniel 2:24–47
What do we learn about Daniel from his response?

_____

_____

_____

Insight

After Babylon conquered Judah, they remained the dominant regional power for several years. Eventually another country, Persia, rose to challenge them. They conquered Babylon and inherited the Jews who had been living in exile—Daniel among them. Daniel, who had been a royal adviser in Babylon, became an adviser to Darius.

THE DECREE OF KING DARIUS
Read Daniel 6:6–15
Why do you think Daniel responds to the decree this way?

_____

_____

_____

DANIEL IN THE LIONS' DEN
Read Daniel 6:16–24

What spiritual awareness do you see emerging in the king's life?

_____

_____

_____

Insight
Daniel defied Persian law and submitted to the Persian death penalty. God's deliverance was more than a reward for his steady faith. It was also the divine declaration of Daniel's innocence based on the law of God. The story demonstrates that God's law is to be obeyed above every other.

A SURPRISING LETTER
Read Daniel 6:25–27

What surprising (but happy) ending does this story contain?

_____

_____

_____

Take It Home
In previous situations, Daniel had wisely used a compromise to keep from acting against his beliefs (Daniel 1:11–16). With the decree of Darius, however, he trusted God and refused to alter his prayer habits in any way. It can be difficult to know when to yield and when to stand firm. What do you think determined how Daniel responded in each circumstance? Can you think of a similar example from your own life, big or small? What beliefs and practices are so important that they can never be compromised?

Connecting the Story Line

- The story of Daniel demonstrates how faith in the one true God can sustain a person in the most difficult times. During the exile, many Jews questioned God's faithfulness, but Daniel remained steadfast and left a spiritual legacy far beyond his own life.

- Daniel prophesied that the people's time in Israel would end, and he reminded them that God's Messiah would be coming. Many scholars view Daniel 9:20–27 as a timetable that outlines the exact number of years until Jesus rode into Jerusalem on a donkey (see Matthew 21).

- Daniel lived a life of courage and prophesied about Jesus' coming. He also had much to say about the end times, themes picked up again in 2 Peter, Jude, and Revelation.

DAY 25
JOSEPH, MARY, AND JESUS' BIRTH

SETTING UP THE STORY

The New Testament begins with the presentation of
Jesus' genealogy, dating all the way past King David to
the father of the nation of Israel, Abraham. Jesus' birth
had been predicted and anticipated since Old Testament
times. He would come to reveal Himself not only as
Israel's long-awaited Messiah but also as the incarnate
Son of God, on earth to take away the sins of the world.
However, despite His divine and kingly status, the
humble circumstances of Jesus' birth paved the way for
a ministry that focused on the poor, downtrodden,
and outcasts of society.

If you have time, read the whole story:
Matthew 1–2; Luke 1:26–2:40

AN ANGEL APPEARS TO MARY
Read Luke 1:26–38
Why do you think Mary would be troubled by the angel's
greeting?

_____

_____

_____

What does Mary's response to the angel's news say about
her faith?

_____

_____

_____

JESUS' BIRTH
Read Luke 2:1–7
Why is it significant that Jesus, the King of kings, is born in such lowly circumstances?

_____

_____

_____

Insight
Much of the imagery that has become part of our Christmas and Nativity traditions has been supplied by filling in the gaps in the Gospel accounts. We are told that there was not room in the inn, though in this case *inn* probably referred to a guest room. It was customary for Jews to have enough room to accommodate their guests, and Joseph and Mary must have expected as much, though this was not the case. As a result, the baby Jesus was wrapped in rags or strips of cloth and placed in a cattle-feeding trough as a crib. We do not know if Jesus was born in a stable or a cave. The feeding trough could have been borrowed, so the baby might have been born under the stars.

THE SHEPHERDS' VISIT
Read Luke 2:8–20
What do we learn from the shepherds' reaction to the baby?

_____

_____

_____

Critical Observation
One of the Old Testament prophecies that tells of Jesus' coming refers to Him as Emmanuel, which means "God with us." Jesus' humble beginnings allow Him to identify with the shepherds. He seemingly has no roof over His head, no house to dwell in. Neither do the shepherds, who

sleep under the stars as they care for their flocks (Luke 2:8). Jesus is poor and of no reputation, as are they. It is additionally fitting that shepherds were some of the first to see Him, as later in life Jesus will be called both the Lamb of God (John 1:29) and the Good Shepherd (John 10:14), images that highlight important parts of Jesus' identity as Savior and Lord.

THE VISIT OF THE MAGI
Read Matthew 2:1–12
How do the magi (or wise men) view Jesus differently than King Herod does?

_____

_____

_____

Insight
The magi were not Jews and may have been wealthy Persian astrologers. With the visit of the magi, Matthew introduces a major theme that he will develop throughout his Gospel: Those whom you would expect to welcome and worship Jesus do not. Instead, Jesus receives homage from those you would least expect to worship Him.

THE FLIGHT TO EGYPT
Read Matthew 2:13–23
Why do you think Herod feels so threatened by Jesus?

_____

_____

_____

Take It Home

When people put God first in their lives, they can expect benefits—and problems as well. Mary and Joseph had the unique privilege of raising the Savior of the world, yet they found themselves homeless in Bethlehem and later pursued by King Herod and forced to flee all the way to Egypt. Their life was not easy. In a similar way, those who choose to follow God today sometimes experience opposition.

Connecting the Story Line

- Jesus makes an unlikely entrance into the world. He wasn't born in a king's court or in a rich man's home. He was born alongside animals. His first visitors were shepherds who belonged to the lower classes of society.

- When Jesus grows up, His ministry will reflect events similar to those surrounding His birth. He reaches out to the poor and disenfranchised while the leaders of His people persecute Him. As with the magi, Jesus often finds the greatest faith among those who are not Jewish.

DAY 26
A YOUNG JESUS IN THE TEMPLE

SETTING UP THE STORY
Certain ceremonies were required after the birth of a child in Jesus' time. If the child was a boy, he would be circumcised on the eighth day and given a name. Jesus, like John the Baptist, was a special case, as an angel of the Lord had previously instructed His parents to specially name Him. After the circumcision, the child would also be presented at the temple and consecrated to the Lord. It is during this ceremony that Mary and Joseph encounter both Simeon and the prophetess Anna, old and devout believers in God who, by the Holy Spirit, testify to God's faithfulness through Jesus and His coming work as Savior.

If you have time, read the whole story: Luke 2:21–52

JESUS PRESENTED IN THE TEMPLE
Read Luke 2:21–24

With Mary and Joseph's close attention to keeping the Jewish law, what do we learn about the family in which Jesus grows up?

_____

_____

_____

Insight
Jesus' name was predetermined and had been announced by Gabriel (Luke 1:31). The Hebrew form of the name was Jeshua, formed by combining two root words that mean "the Lord" and "to save." Thus Jesus' name literally means "the Lord is salvation."

GOD'S PROMISE TO SIMEON
Read Luke 2:25–38
Why does Simeon praise God?

_____

_____

_____

How does Simeon describe the baby Jesus?

_____

_____

_____

Insight
The testimonies of Simeon and Anna confirm Jesus' identity as Israel's Messiah. Note that we are only told about Simeon and Anna's proclamations; we don't have any record of the rituals performed at the temple for Jesus' consecration. The announcements of God's faithfulness and Jesus' true identity are the important events at this time, not the formal rituals.

Critical Observation
Luke fast-forwards twelve years to tell another story of Jesus at the temple in Luke 2:41–52. It is the only biblical account in the life of Jesus between His birth and His adult ministry. Mary and Joseph, like all devout Jews, traveled annually to Jerusalem to observe the Passover. During one of their visits, they accidentally began their trip home to Nazareth without Jesus. After returning to Jerusalem, they discovered Him in the temple, sitting with the teachers and learning. Jesus' response, His earliest recorded words in the Gospels, reflects His love for God and His burgeoning understanding of His own identity.

THE BOY JESUS AT THE TEMPLE

Read Luke 2:41–52

What is so surprising about this episode from Jesus' life?

_____

_____

_____

Which traits of Jesus are being revealed at a young age?

_____

_____

_____

What do you think it means when Mary is said to have "kept all these sayings in her heart" (Luke 2:51)?

_____

_____

_____

Take It Home

Jesus honored His earthly parents and was obedient to them (Luke 2:51), yet He also recognized His true identity and calling as the Lord's Servant, the Messiah, and the Son of God. He understood His ultimate priorities. Later in life, Jesus calls His disciples to the same high standard when He says, "He that loveth father or mother more than me is not worthy of me" (Matthew 10:37). Clearly Jesus wants His disciples to love and honor their parents. However, He also challenges them to give Him their ultimate allegiance. We should not love anything or anyone as much as we love the Lord. What place does God have in your heart?

Connecting the Story Line

- In these chapters, we see Jesus beginning to grow physically, emotionally, and spiritually in preparation for His divinely appointed ministry.

- This story establishes the vital Father/Son relationship between God the Father and Jesus His Son. All four Gospels frequently highlight this status, and it is how we understand Jesus as the second person of the Trinity.

DAY 27
THE MINISTRY OF JOHN THE BAPTIST

SETTING UP THE STORY
After the miraculous account of his birth (Luke 1), John the Baptist grows up to have a powerful ministry proclaiming the coming of the kingdom of heaven while pointing all his followers to Jesus, the true Messiah. However, his life is not without trouble, and he—like Jesus' disciples—struggles to have faith in what he doesn't see or understand.

If you have time, read the whole story:
Matthew 3:1–17; 11:1–15; 14:1–12

JOHN THE BAPTIST PREPARES THE WAY
Read Luke 3:1–20
List the things John the Baptist tells people to do and not to do. What is the main point behind these ideas?

_____

_____

_____

Critical Observation
John begins preaching in the wilderness with this message: Repent and look toward the kingdom of God, which is near (Matthew 3:2). Though short, this message holds great theological significance. Jesus Himself would preach the same message during His ministry (Matthew 4:17).

THE BAPTISM OF JESUS
Read Matthew 3:13–17
What do we learn about Jesus' identity and relationship with the Father at His baptism?

_____

_____

_____

JOHN QUESTIONS JESUS
Read Matthew 11:1–15

What does Jesus say about John and his calling?

_____

_____

_____

Insight

When John baptizes Jesus, God immediately gives His approval. We see the activity of the Holy Spirit in the life and ministry of Jesus, reinforcing this aspect of divine intervention. Jesus' baptism plays a significant role in affirming both His sonship and His status, fulfilling two major Old Testament prophecies: Psalm 2:7 (Jesus as God's Son) and Isaiah 42:1 (Jesus as God's Servant).

JOHN IS BEHEADED
Read Matthew 14:1–12

What does Herod mistakenly think about John, and why?

_____

_____

_____

What does this story reveal about Herod's character?

_____

_____

_____

Insight

The Herod in this story is not Herod the Great from the narrative of Jesus' birth (Luke 2). This is his son, Herod Antipas. John the Baptist had condemned Herod Antipas because he had married his half brother Philip's wife. One can see how the patterns of unbelief and sinful living have carried on from father to son.

The kingdom of God that both John and Jesus speak of is a kingdom that resides outside of this world. How does the news of John's death illustrate this fact?

_____

_____

_____

Take It Home

Early in his ministry, John the Baptist passionately preached that the kingdom of heaven was at hand. He knew that his calling was from the Lord. When Jesus arrived, he recognized Him as the prophesied Messiah (John 1:29–31). However, he was soon thrown in prison by Herod Antipas, where he would eventually die before seeing Jesus crucified and raised from the dead. It would have been natural to question and doubt. What John needed, and what he ultimately had, was faith not in what is seen but in what is unseen (see Hebrews 11:1). In what ways do you struggle in your faith? What might the story of John have to say to you?

Connecting the Story Line

- The kingdom of God is a theme preached by John the Baptist. Ultimately, it shows that God is more concerned about the hearts of His people than with possession of the land of Israel. When Jesus arrived, He was not interested in casting off the oppressive Roman rulers who held power in the land. Instead of leading a military revolution, He spoke to the hearts of people.

- The lives of John and Jesus represent the culmination of all the prophets who came before them in the Old Testament (see Matthew 11:13).

DAY 28
THE TEACHINGS OF JESUS

SETTING UP THE STORY

Jesus is most well known for the things He accomplished during His life, not only in the cross and resurrection, but also in the miracles He did beforehand, such as the feeding of the five thousand and the healing of the blind and sick. However, Jesus also spent considerable time teaching His disciples and the crowds what it meant to love God and live for Him. His teachings are vital to understanding His ministry, and they have been passed down for centuries as the basis for the most important doctrines of the church.

If you have time, read the whole story:
Matthew, Mark, Luke, and John

THE BEATITUDES
Read Matthew 5:1–12

List some characteristics that Jesus describes, rewriting them in your own words. How can you live these out in your own life?

_____

_____

_____

Critical Observation

Matthew 5 is commonly called "the Beatitudes." Here are a few important notes about these famous verses in scripture:

- They address the character of those who would follow Christ.
- They stress the radical nature of Christian discipleship.
- The blessedness they promise is a deep, inner spiritual richness, not a superficial happiness.

THE GREATEST COMMANDMENT
Read Mark 12:28–34

In what ways could each of the Ten Commandments found in Exodus 20 be summarized by Jesus' two commands here?

_____

_____

_____

DO NOT WORRY
Read Luke 12:22–34

How would you summarize the meaning of these verses to a friend who is under great stress?

_____

_____

_____

Insight

Jesus' teaching on worry is all about perspective. When we understand how well He provides for all His creation, our worries become a littler smaller in comparison. God does not promise that our lives will be easy, but He does promise to provide us with what we need. When we worry about clothing or food, we fail to focus on what is most important in life.

THE BREAD OF LIFE AND LIVING WATER
Read John 6:32–40; 7:37–39

What do you think is Jesus' point in comparing physical food and spiritual food?

_____

_____

_____

Why do you suppose Jesus compares the Holy Spirit to streams of water?

_____

_____

_____

Insight

Jesus' statement "I am the bread of life" (John 6:35) takes on extra meaning in light of the Last Supper. During Jesus' last meal with His disciples before the Crucifixion, He breaks bread and says, "This is my body which is given for you" (Luke 22:19). To partake with Jesus is to accept His death on the cross for our sins and participate with Him in His suffering.

THE LITTLE CHILDREN
Read Matthew 19:13–15
Why does Jesus make time for blessing children?

_____

_____

_____

Take It Home

Much of Jesus' ministry and teaching is centered around the concept of love. The well-known verse John 3:16 says, "For God so loved the world, that he gave his only begotten Son, that whosoever believeth in him should not perish, but have everlasting life." Jesus Himself says that the greatest commandments are to "love the Lord thy God with all thy heart, and with all thy soul, and with all thy mind, and with all thy strength" and to "love thy neighbour as thyself" (Mark 12:30–31). God loves us perfectly and fully, and He asks us to love Him and others in return. How can you better display your love for Him? How might you better demonstrate love for others?

Connecting the Story Line

- Jesus often quoted the Old Testament in His teachings. The Law and Prophets pointed to His coming as the true Messiah of Israel. He also taught how the heart of God can be known through the Old Testament.

- Jesus' teachings revealed the character of God to His disciples. His message became the foundation for the early church and for the church today.

DAY 29
THE MIRACLES OF JESUS

SETTING UP THE STORY
The miracles that Jesus performs in the four Gospels tell us much about His true nature and identity as both Messiah and Son of God. Many of His actions indicate the presence of the kingdom of God in the world. Jesus is Israel's long-awaited Messiah, the Christ, and His miracles confirm this identity (Isaiah 35:5; 61:1). They also demonstrate His power over pain, sickness, death, the natural world, and the spiritual realm. Jesus does things that only God can do, proving that He is both Lord and King.

If you have time, read the whole story:
Matthew, Mark, Luke, and John

JESUS FEEDS THE FIVE THOUSAND
Read Matthew 14:13–21
In what way does this remind you that elsewhere Jesus refers to Himself as "the bread of life"?

_____

_____

_____

What does this episode say about the faith of the disciples?

_____

_____

_____

Critical Observation
The feeding of the five thousand is the only miracle recorded in all four Gospels (Matthew 14:13–21; Mark 6:30–44; Luke 9:10–17; John 6:1–13). It indicates that Jesus, as God's Messiah, can take care of His people.

There is a clear connection to the feeding of the people of Israel with manna in the wilderness after they left Egypt (Exodus 16:3–4). The miracle also brings to mind the prophetic image of the messianic banquet at the end of time, in which God's redeemed will sit with Him at the table and enjoy a banquet together (Revelation 19:9).

JESUS WALKS ON WATER
Read Matthew 14:22–32
What do you learn about Jesus from this story?

_____

_____

_____

JESUS HEALS A DEMON-POSSESSED MAN
Read Mark 5:1–20
What is the significance of the demons' fear of Jesus?

_____

_____

_____

JESUS CALMS THE STORM
Read Luke 8:22–25
What does Jesus' power over the storm reveal?

_____

_____

_____

Insight
In calming the wind and the waves, Jesus did something that only God could do. The psalmist says of God, "He maketh the storm a calm, so that the waves thereof are still" (Psalm 107:29). By calming the storm as He did, Jesus was showing His disciples that He is God.

JESUS HEALS A MAN BORN BLIND
Read John 9:1–12

What does this story reveal about Jesus' power over human ailments?

_____

_____

_____

Why is it significant that Jesus performs miracles? What do His miracles tell you about Him?

_____

_____

_____

Take It Home

Jesus' miracles were frequently met with opposition, whether from the Pharisees and other religious leaders or from regular townspeople. These people were often resistant to change and became upset because Jesus challenged the status quo. Are you open to God's work in your life, even if it isn't always comfortable?

Connecting the Story Line

- These miracles demonstrate Jesus' divinity. As God Himself, Jesus possesses ultimate power and authority over creation and the laws of nature.

- Revelation 21 tells how God will make everything perfect when He institutes a new earth. The healings Jesus does during His earthly ministry serve as a foreshadowing of what is to come.

DAY 30
JESUS AND LAZARUS

SETTING UP THE STORY

Jesus had a friend named Lazarus who had two sisters, Martha and Mary. A unique story occurs in Jesus' ministry when Lazarus dies. It's more than a miracle story—it's also one of faith. The disciples believe that Jesus is going to die when He goes back to Judea, but they resolutely follow Him. The sisters of Lazarus believe that death has conquered their brother. Clearly, it has not yet occurred to anyone that Jesus' power is greater than death.

If you have time, read the whole story: John 11:1–57

THE DEATH OF LAZARUS
Read John 11:1–6
What does it mean to you that John says Jesus loved Lazarus and knew him personally?

_____

_____

_____

Insight
Lazarus is noted as someone Jesus loved (John 11:3). They had a close relationship. Jesus had previously healed others whom He had never met, so it would have been natural for the disciples, as well as Mary and Martha, to expect Jesus to heal a man who meant so much to Him.

JESUS COMFORTS THE SISTERS
Read John 11:17–37

What do the comments of Martha, Mary, and the other onlookers reveal about their faith?

_____

_____

_____

What do you think it means that Jesus weeps after hearing that Lazarus has died?

_____

_____

_____

Insight
The four days Lazarus's body was in the tomb (John 11:17) were sufficient to confirm that he was dead. As was custom at the time, relatives and neighbors would have come to care for the family in their time of grief. Frequently a funeral band would also have been hired. There would thus have been a large gathering of people, all mourning with the grieving family.

Critical Observation
John 11:4 is key to this story. Jesus declares that Lazarus's sickness will not result in death. Lazarus will die, but his death will not be final. Rather, the sickness will provide occasion for God to be revealed through the power of Jesus by raising Lazarus from the dead.

In verse 25 we see the lesson of the story. Jesus is changing the focus of the conversation from the eventual resurrection of the dead to the fact that He is the One with power and authority over death. Jesus is the source of resurrection and life (11:25–26).

JESUS RAISES LAZARUS FROM THE DEAD
Read John 11:38–44

Jesus' actions reveal that He has power over life and death. How is this important for the rest of the story of John's Gospel?

_____

_____

_____

REACTION OF THE LEADERS
Read John 11:45–48

What do these verses reveal about the selfish motivation of the leaders who oppose Jesus?

_____

_____

_____

Reread the story of Jesus and Lazarus. List all the attributes of Jesus that are evident in this story.

_____

_____

_____

Take It Home

God is sovereign over all the evils that confront us. He is able to make good come from both good and evil situations. If we experience loss and pain, we can still have faith in God and believe that God alone is worthy of our trust and worship. Jesus' life, ministry, death, and resurrection demonstrate this fact.

Connecting the Story Line

- Mary and Martha were challenged to have faith, even when they did not understand why bad things were happening. The disciples will be challenged to have the same faith in chapter 19, after Jesus is crucified.

- The resurrection of Lazarus proves that Jesus has power over death. It foreshadows the eventual resurrection of Christ Himself, as well as the eventual resurrection of those who believe in Him (see 1 Corinthians 15).

DAY 31
THE PARABLES OF JESUS

SETTING UP THE STORY
Along with His teachings and miracles, Jesus frequently
used parables to communicate His message. Parables are
short stories that illustrate a moral or theological point.
Many of Jesus' parables are concerned with the coming
and future reality of the kingdom of God. Though
parables can often be difficult to understand, Jesus said
that these stories revealed the secrets of the kingdom of
God to His followers (Luke 8:10).

If you have time, read the whole story:
Matthew, Mark, Luke, and John

THE WISE AND FOOLISH BUILDERS
Read Luke 6:46–49
How would you summarize this parable?

_____

_____

_____

THE GOOD SAMARITAN
Read Luke 10:25–37
How does the story of the Good Samaritan challenge you?

_____

_____

_____

Critical Observation
The tension between Jews and Samaritans had existed for
centuries before Jesus' day. When the Assyrians conquered
the northern kingdom of Israel in the mid-700s BC, they
took most Jews into exile and repopulated Samaria with

others. The remaining Israelites eventually intermarried with the Gentiles and abandoned their faith. The Jews who returned from captivity faced opposition from these new inhabitants, creating great tension between Jews and Samaritans. It is thus even more radical that it was a Samaritan who helped the Jewish man, when a priest and a Levite would not.

THE MUSTARD SEED AND THE YEAST
Read Luke 13:18–21
In what ways is the kingdom of God like a mustard seed?

_____
_____
_____

Jesus says that the kingdom of God is also like yeast. What does that illustration teach you about God's kingdom?

_____
_____
_____

THE LOST SHEEP
Read Luke 15:4–7
What insight into God does this parable provide?

_____
_____
_____

THE PRODIGAL SON
Read Luke 15:11–32
Describe how each brother responds to the father. What mistakes does each make?

_____
_____
_____

Insight

Sometimes the parable of the prodigal son is read primarily as a source of comfort for parents with wayward children, and in one sense it is. However, this parable was told to shock the readers with the unconditional love and grace of the father.

THE TEN MINAS

Read Luke 19:11–27

What is the lesson of this parable?

_____

_____

_____

Take It Home

The characters in the parables were normal people—carpenters, servants, fathers, sons, travelers. These stories were designed to be real-world applications of Jesus' kingdom teachings. They were practical, not theoretical. Many times in the church today, we make a false distinction between what we believe and what we do, but for Jesus and the other New Testament writers, there was no such distinction. Jesus calls us to believe in Him and let that belief permeate every part of our lives. Our faith and actions should be intimately connected. Do you struggle sometimes to live out what you believe? Are your actions different than your faith? How might you bridge the gap between words and deeds?

Connecting the Story Line

- Jesus' parables dealt with holy living in the world, the exact concern that the early church would face in their societies and that we still face today.

- The parables tell us not only about Jesus' moral teaching but also about the present and future realities of the kingdom of God.

Day 32
Palm Sunday and the Last Supper

Setting Up the Story
After three years of ministry throughout Jerusalem and Galilee, Jesus enters His final week before the Crucifixion. According to tradition and the Gospel accounts, Jesus triumphantly enters Jerusalem on a Sunday, is crucified the following Friday, and rises from the dead the next Sunday. Though the disciples do not yet understand the profound nature of the events that are about to occur, Jesus is painfully and fully aware of what awaits Him.

If you have time, read the whole story:
Matthew 21:1–11; 26:17–35

The Disciples Prepare to Enter Jerusalem
Read Matthew 21:1–6
Why does Jesus enter Jerusalem the way He does?

_____

_____

_____

The Triumphal Entry
Read Matthew 21:7–11
Describe the crowd's response to Jesus.

_____

_____

_____

Insight
Jesus' entry into Jerusalem is a turning point in the Gospel narrative. It marks the end of His ministry in Galilee and begins the tragic passion narrative. (The week leading up to Jesus' death is often called "Passion Week.") Though the triumphal entry honors Jesus, it is nonetheless with a mixture of truth and irony. It is this same crowd that will be screaming, "Let Him be crucified!" less than one week later.

THE DISCIPLES PREPARE FOR THE LAST SUPPER
Read Matthew 26:17–20
What does Jesus say that reveals He knows that His death is near?

_____

_____

_____

JESUS PREDICTS JUDAS'S BETRAYAL
Read Matthew 26:21–25
If Jesus knows of Judas's plans, why doesn't He put a stop to them?

_____

_____

_____

Insight
Jesus' stern warning regarding the one who will betray Him probably confused and unsettled the disciples. They most likely did not understand. Jesus understood, however, that the betrayal was in fulfillment of prophecy. He needed to be betrayed in order to be crucified in order to release the world from sin.

THE LAST SUPPER
Read Matthew 26:26–30
What do the bread and wine represent?

_____

_____

_____

What is the significance of Jesus sharing many of His last moments on earth with His disciples?

_____

_____

_____

Critical Observation

The Last Supper actually occurred during a Passover meal, the annual Jewish celebration in memory of the Passover and Exodus from Egypt. During the first Passover, the Lord commanded all the Israelites to spread the blood of a lamb on their doorposts so that the angel of the Lord would pass over their houses and not kill their firstborn sons. This is a fitting analogy since the Bible has already identified Jesus as the ultimate Lamb of God, whose death will save all who believe in Him. It is no coincidence that His death takes place during the Passover celebration.

THE BETRAYAL
Read Matthew 26:36–50
Describe Jesus' behavior as He prepares to be crucified. What does this tell us about Him?

_____

_____

_____

Take It Home

During the Last Supper, Jesus knew that He was soon going to be crucified. His death would be excruciatingly slow and painful. Even so, Jesus did not run, hide, or attempt to evade His fate. He was aware that His entire life and ministry had been building to this point and were going to culminate in the next few days.

Jesus calls us to take up our crosses and follow Him (Matthew 16:24–25). While this doesn't mean we should literally be crucified, it does paint a picture of total sacrifice for the sake of Christ. Are you willing to follow Jesus even when it's painful or uncomfortable? What can you learn from Jesus' faith in the days leading up to the cross?

Connecting the Story Line

- The Triumphal Entry is still celebrated in the church today on the Sunday before Easter, in recognition of Jesus' preparation for Passion Week. In many churches it is called "Palm Sunday."

- Jesus' Last Supper instituted the practice of communion, which is still an integral part of worship in churches today.

- Holy Communion (also called the Eucharist) provides us with another picture of Christ's sacrificial death and also a way to participate with Him in it.

Day 33
Jesus' Death on the Cross

Setting Up the Story
Jesus moves toward the culmination of His earthly ministry, which is the means by which salvation will be brought to humanity. His death on the cross is in fulfillment of God's plan, not a result of Pilate's power or the Jews' scheming. Though others try to control Jesus and achieve their own purposes, God remains in control the entire time. Jesus' death and resurrection are God's rescue plan for the world.

If you have time, read the whole story: John 18–19

Jesus Arrested
Read John 18:1–11
What is Jesus' attitude about being arrested?

_____

_____

_____

Peter's Three Denials
Read John 18:15–18, 25–27
Why do you think Peter denies Christ?

_____

_____

_____

Insight
Peter goes from the height of passion in defending Jesus (Matthew 26:33) to the depths of despair in denying Him three times. Though he experienced a range of passion, it doesn't seem that he truly trusted Jesus to know what was best.

JESUS TALKS TO PILATE
Read John 18:29–40
How does Jesus describe His purpose to Pilate?

_____

_____

_____

Insight
The Jews had already complained once to Caesar about Pilate's actions in another conflict. Pilate feared he might lose his position if the Jews complained again and accused him of failing to deal with an insurrection. Though he tried to avoid making a decision about Jesus, Pilate ultimately acted out of fear and ordered Jesus to be crucified.

JESUS SENTENCED TO BE CRUCIFIED
Read John 19:1–16
Why do the Jews think Jesus should be crucified?

_____

_____

_____

THE CRUCIFIXION
Read John 19:17–30
What does Jesus' suffering teach about the seriousness of sin and His love for humanity?

_____

_____

_____

Critical Observation
Crucifixion was a Roman form of execution and torture, a slow and enormously painful way to die. Victims could hang on the cross for several days before finally passing away. To speed up this process, Roman soldiers often broke the legs of the one being crucified. As the person hung on the cross, it became increasingly difficult to breathe, and he

would have to push up on his legs in order to gain a breath. Remember, his feet would be pierced, and his back, already raw from flogging, would scrape against the wooden cross. Breaking his legs would take away any ability to support himself in order to breathe, and death would come a little more quickly. Thus, to die by crucifixion was ultimately to die by asphyxiation.

Even in His final recorded breaths, Jesus is focused on others. What do the events of John 19:25–27 reveal of Jesus' limitless compassion?

_____

_____

_____

Take It Home
The role of Pilate and the Jews in the crucifixion story reminds us that we all have to face the same question: What are we going to do with Jesus? Will we trade Him for someone more like us? Will we wash our hands of Him rather than deal with the demands He makes on our lives? Or will we acknowledge His true identity and surrender our lives to Him? This is the most important decision you will ever face in life. Have you made it?

Connecting the Story Line

- Jesus' death and subsequent resurrection are the source of salvation for all who believe in Him. These events are foundational to the life of the church.

- Jesus' death ultimately demonstrates God's unending love for humanity.

- Jesus' death is in fulfillment of many Old Testament prophecies from the Law, Prophets, and Psalms.

DAY 34
THE RESURRECTION

SETTING UP THE STORY
According to tradition and the Gospels, Jesus was crucified and buried on a Friday. His disciples and followers are left scattered, confused, and distraught. Until this moment, they have been expecting Jesus to literally and physically restore the kingdom to Israel, and His death is both surprising and disheartening. When Mary Magdalene returns to visit Jesus' tomb on Sunday, she finds it empty.

If you have time, read the whole story: John 20–21

THE EMPTY TOMB
Read John 20:1–9
What does Mary Magdalene initially think happened to Jesus?

_____

_____

_____

Insight
The empty tomb and subsequent appearances are evidence of not only a spiritual resurrection but also a physical one. Jesus didn't rise as a spirit but as a living human being.

JESUS APPEARS TO MARY MAGDALENE
Read John 20:10–18
What is surprising about the fact that Jesus appears first to a woman?

_____

_____

_____

Church tradition describes Mary Magdalene as a very sinful woman before she met Jesus. What would be the significance of Jesus' first post-resurrection appearance to someone with a sordid past?

_____

_____

_____

Critical Observation

Women were low on the totem pole in the social world of the first century. Jesus' appearance to Mary Magdalene, entrusting her to be the first person to spread the good news of His resurrection, is a sign of validation for women and the socially limited. This is very consistent with the rest of Jesus' ministry, in which He frequently reached out to and loved the outcasts and marginalized in society.

JESUS APPEARS TO THE DISCIPLES
Read John 20:19–29

How would you describe Jesus' interaction with "doubting Thomas" in this story?

_____

_____

_____

Insight

Jesus lays out a principle for His followers: It is one thing to have seen Jesus and believe, yet it is a greater thing to believe without ever having seen the resurrected Christ. Since Jesus' day, countless people have believed without seeing. Their trust in the Word of God is real, undeniable faith.

JESUS REINSTATES PETER
Read John 21:15–19

Why do you think Jesus does this?

_____

_____

_____

What makes the Resurrection so significant to the Christian faith?

_____

_____

_____

Take It Home

Many people are uncertain about death and view it as a frightening and mysterious unknown. Their solution often is to simply not think about it. However, the Bible teaches that "death is the destiny of every man; the living should take this to heart" (Ecclesiastes 7:2 NIV). And the resurrection narrative demonstrates God's ultimate mastery over death. Christians can rest assured that we will live with God when we die. As we look forward to the resurrection of the dead at Christ's second coming, we do not live without hope.

Connecting the Story Line

- The Resurrection is the exalted apex of the Bible's story line. By His resurrection, Jesus defeats sin, death, and the devil, allowing those who follow Him to live free lives for God's glory.

- Jesus serves as the final solution to problems that Adam and Eve created through their disobedience in the Garden of Eden (Genesis 3; Romans 5).

- Jesus' resurrection provides the basis for an understanding of our future resurrection as believers in Christ (1 Corinthians 15).

Day 35
Pentecost and the Arrival of the Holy Spirit

Setting Up the Story
Prior to His crucifixion, Jesus told His followers that the Holy Spirit would come to replace Him after His departure (John 14:15–27; 16:5–16). Before He ascended to heaven after His resurrection, Jesus instructed them to go to Jerusalem and await the Holy Spirit (Acts 1:4). The coming of the Spirit (on the day of Pentecost) unmistakably transformed the community of believers and began the rapid growth of the church.

If you have time, read the whole story: Acts 2:1–47

A Sight, a Sound, and Strange Speech
Read Acts 2:1–13
What languages are the apostles speaking?

_____

_____

_____

Insight
The celebration of Pentecost, known as the Feast of Harvest or Feast of Weeks, was the middle of three annual Jewish harvest festivals. It also came to be celebrated as the anniversary of the giving of the law at Mount Sinai, since Sinai came roughly fifty days after the Exodus and Pentecost came fifty days after Passover. It is no coincidence that God fulfilled His promise on that day. While the people were ready to celebrate the harvest, God was ready for a harvest of a different sort (Luke 10:2). And the sound, fire, and speech present at Sinai were present once again at Pentecost.

PETER'S EXPLANATION
Read Acts 2:14–15, 29–36

To whom is Peter speaking? In what ways does he direct his message toward his audience?

_____

_____

_____

How has Peter changed from what we saw of him during Jesus' crucifixion? To what would you attribute the change?

_____

_____

_____

Critical Observation

One might wonder how Peter became a source of such profound spiritual insight and theological acuity in that he was able to recognize Jesus as the fulfillment of so many Old Testament prophecies. Perhaps a clue is found in the story of the two disciples on the road to Emmaus (Luke 24:13–35). As Jesus walked with them, "beginning at Moses and all the prophets, he expounded unto them in all the scriptures the things concerning himself" (Luke 24:27). Likewise, Jesus spent numerous occasions with His disciples after His resurrection discussing the kingdom of God (Acts 1:3). In light of the Resurrection, the apostles began to better understand what had happened and why. And with the presence and power of the Holy Spirit, Peter was able to concisely summarize the facts and persuade his listeners.

THE PEOPLE'S RESPONSE
Read Acts 2:37–41

What does Peter say is the appropriate response to his message?

_____

_____

_____

How many people accept Peter's message and are baptized that day?

_____

_____

_____

Insight

In one day, church membership increased twenty-five times its original number, and more people were added every day (Acts 2:47). In a modern setting, such growth might create problems, yet in its earliest stages, it seemed that the new and growing church was doing everything right. It was a model in worship, discipleship, caring for others, evangelizing, and serving.

THE FIRST CHURCH
Acts 2:42–47

What actions and attitudes mark the members of the first church?

_____

_____

_____

Take It Home

Today's church encounters many of the same challenges that the first-century church faced. Many people do not understand Christian beliefs and are distrustful or even hostile toward the church. In some countries, Christians are persecuted with the same cruel intolerance that the members of the early church were soon to face. What can be done collectively to make your body of believers stronger? What might you do personally to make a difference?

Connecting the Story Line

- The coming of the Holy Spirit propelled the church forward into new growth. The rest of the book of Acts testifies to the Spirit's work in establishing and sustaining the church. This same Spirit is alive and active in the church today.

- At Pentecost God fulfills two significant promises: that He would send His Spirit (Ezekiel 36:27) and that He would write His law on the hearts and minds of His people (Jeremiah 31:33).

Day 36
Saul/Paul's Conversion

Setting Up the Story

Jesus had told His followers that they would be His witnesses in Jerusalem, Judea, Samaria, and to the ends of the earth (Acts 1:8). Until the church realized its first martyr, Stephen, the Christians had remained a small community in Jerusalem. The outbreak of persecution drove the church in all directions and allowed them to spread the gospel more rapidly in diverse locations. Saul, who would later become the apostle Paul, was at first a persecutor of the church, before God intervened in his life and he became one of the gospel's most passionate defenders.

If you have time, read the whole story:
Acts 7:54–9:31; 13–28

Saul Persecutes the Church
Read Acts 7:54–8:3

What is Stephen's response to his inevitable martyrdom?

_____

_____

_____

What do we learn about Saul in this first encounter with him?

_____

_____

_____

SAUL ON THE ROAD TO DAMASCUS
Read Acts 9:1–9
What does Saul's conversion tell us about God?

_____

_____

_____

Why do you suppose Jesus appears to Saul in such a drastic fashion?

_____

_____

_____

Critical Observation
The trip to Damascus was a serious commitment. The city was about 150 miles from Jerusalem—a journey that would require almost a week by foot. Because many Jews lived in Damascus, the synagogues would have been a good place to seek out converts to the new Christian religion. Saul demonstrated passion in his desire to stamp out Christianity, passion that would be rededicated after his conversion.

GOD'S INSTRUCTIONS FOR ANANIAS
Read Acts 9:10–19
Do you think Ananias should be afraid of Saul? What do his actions say about his faith?

_____

_____

_____

Insight

Saul had become notorious for his persecution of Christianity, and Ananias had heard of his misdeeds (Acts 9:13–14). Saul had not yet shown any outward signs of conversion, so it would have taken tremendous faith for Ananias to actually seek Saul out and speak with him.

SAUL BECOMES A MISSIONARY
Read Acts 9:19–31
How do the disciples respond to Saul?

_____

_____

_____

Insight

In Jerusalem, after his conversion, Saul was a man with no place to go. He wanted to unite with the other Christians, but they did not know what had happened to him on the way to Damascus. He needed someone to reach out to him. That person turned out to be Barnabas, who was nicknamed the "Son of Encouragement." Barnabas might have received a special word from the Lord, but we aren't told so. Perhaps he just recognized that it was right to give someone a chance for repentance and forgiveness.

What does the story of Saul tell us about grace and forgiveness?

_____

_____

_____

Take It Home

Saul (Paul) played a tremendously important role in the life of the early church, yet twice in the early stages of his faith, it was other people who played the important role in helping him find his place. Ananias and Barnabas are not often recognized for their contributions, but their fearless service should not go unnoticed. The church is always in need of those unsung servants who will go outside their comfort zones to guide and encourage those who need to know more about Jesus. What unique opportunities has God given you?

Connecting the Story Line

- Saul, later known as Paul, becomes one of the most significant missionaries in Christian history. He also writes many of the letters that end up in the New Testament (Paul wrote the New Testament from Romans through Philemon).

- Saul's conversion perfectly illustrates God's all-encompassing grace. It also demonstrates that new life in Christ is open to all, even those who seem most unlikely to receive it.

Day 37
Paul's Epistles

Setting Up the Story

Though Paul's early life was spent persecuting the church, his dramatic conversion on the road to Damascus transformed him into one of Christianity's most passionate missionaries and defenders of the faith. He took three separate, lengthy missionary journeys throughout the eastern Mediterranean world, traveling as far west as Rome, to establish churches in areas that were previously unfamiliar with the gospel. Paul made it a habit to keep in contact with these churches afterward, to encourage and guide them through any potential problems. While he occasionally visited in person, he often wrote letters (also called epistles), which were delivered by assistants or fellow missionaries during their own travels. We still have many of these letters to churches in cities like Rome, Corinth, Ephesus, and Philippi, and they form a large portion of the New Testament canon.

If you have time, read the whole story: Romans–Philemon

More Than Conquerors
Read Romans 8:28–39
How does Paul encourage the Christians in Rome to respond to God's goodness?

_____

_____

_____

Insight
God's people will suffer, just as Jesus did, yet He is with us through every painful ordeal. Romans 8:38–39 shows us the limitless reach of God's love for us. There is nothing that can separate us from His love. We have total security in the midst of our trials.

JUSTIFICATION BY FAITH
Read Galatians 2:15–21
Why do you think Paul reminds the church in Galatia about the basis of unity for both Jews and Gentiles?

_____

_____

_____

Critical Observation
Paul is not just making a theological argument here but is also speaking personally about a God who lovingly gave His life for us (Galatians 2:20). It is one thing to theoretically believe that God died for the sins of the world, but quite another to comprehend that He died for each individual in order that they might have a personal and loving relationship with Him. With this knowledge, we can experience a more intense passion and joy in response to God's gift of salvation.

SALVATION BY GRACE
Read Ephesians 2:1–10
What truth does Paul need to remind the Ephesians about regarding their salvation?

_____

_____

_____

HOLY LIVING IN THE LIGHT OF CHRIST
Read Philippians 2:1–11
Who does Paul remind the Philippians to imitate? Why?

_____

_____

_____

Insight
The traditional title for Philippians 2:5–11 is *Carmen Christi*, or the "Hymn of Christ." Many scholars think that these verses were not original to Paul but were instead a citation from an already existing Christian hymn. These words would have been known and repeated in churches everywhere in recognition of Christ's lordship.

THE SUPREMACY OF CHRIST
Read Colossians 1:15–23
List some of the attributes of Jesus from this letter to the Colossians.

_____

_____

_____

What themes have you seen in these samplings of Paul's work?

_____

_____

_____

Take It Home

Earlier in his life, Paul was one of the last people anyone would expect to become a follower of Christ. God, however, had other plans for him. God used Paul to spread the gospel and encourage the church. Because of Paul's letters in the New Testament, his influence continues to be felt today. God's gracious plan is so much greater than anything we can imagine.

Connecting the Story Line

• Paul and the other apostles elaborated on and spread the teachings of Jesus after His death and resurrection. Paul's teaching offered stability for the early church, and his work continues to be essential in expressing church doctrine today.

• Paul was one of the first to address problems specific to local churches, and his practical advice continues to be valuable for churches around the world.

DAY 38
THE BOOK OF HEBREWS

SETTING UP THE STORY
No one can say with certainty who wrote the book of Hebrews. While some believe it was Paul, others like to suggest other Bible characters such as Barnabas, Luke, or Apollos. Regardless, we know that the recipients of the letter were Jewish Christians. They had been suffering for their faith and were likely beginning to waver, tempted to return to their old, familiar way of life. Hebrews is a challenge and an encouragement, then, reminding its readers of the supremacy of Christ over everything, Jewish or Gentile, and encouraging believers to stand firm because of their new identities in Jesus.

If you have time, read the whole story: Hebrews 1–13

JESUS IS GREATER THAN MOSES
Read Hebrews 3:1–6
In what ways is Jesus like Moses? How is He unlike Moses?

_____

_____

_____

Insight
Some might see these passages in Hebrews as disparaging Moses and the Old Testament, but that is clearly not what the author has in mind. Moses was a faithful prophet and servant of the Lord, but Jesus' work of salvation deserves greater honor. Moses isn't lowered at all. Jesus, on the other hand, is elevated.

JESUS LIKE MELCHIZEDEK
Read Hebrews 7:11–22
How is the new covenant "better" than the old one?

_____

_____

_____

Critical Observation
The Bible says very little about the person of Melchizedek, though the author of Hebrews apparently assumed that his readers were familiar with him. He is only mentioned in scripture in Genesis 14:18–20, where Abraham pays him great honor. Melchizedek, whose name means "king of righteousness," was said to be the king of Salem and a priest of God Most High. While some scholars believe his appearance in Genesis was a preincarnate appearance of Christ Himself, scripture only says that Jesus was like him, not that they were the same person. The author's ultimate point is that Jesus' priesthood is not in the line of the Levites, which would have put Him under the Mosaic Law, but is rather a new thing from a new line. Jesus is doing fresh, new work.

JESUS, THE PERFECT HIGH PRIEST
Read Hebrews 7:23–28
Why does the high priest need to be set apart from others?

_____

_____

_____

What does it mean that Jesus will forever be a priest who intercedes for us?

_____

_____

_____

RESPONDING TO CHRIST
Read Hebrews 10:19–25
Because of Christ, how can we view God? What about each other?

_____

_____

_____

NOTEWORTHY FAITH
Read Hebrews 11:29–40
How does the author conclude this section on faith? What does that mean for us?

_____

_____

_____

Insight
By highlighting the faith of so many different biblical heroes, the author of Hebrews not only provides his readers with wonderful examples to follow but also demonstrates that the faithful in both the Old and New Testaments ultimately drew near to God by faith, not sacrifice or ceremony.

In what ways do you find that the book of Hebrews connects the Old and New Testaments?

_____

_____

_____

Take It Home

Many of the images and concepts in the book of Hebrews are unfamiliar to us. The church today no longer offers sacrifices or participates in any of the other rituals common for Jews in the Old Testament. However, this does not keep us from seeing the author's ultimate point—namely, that Jesus is the Lord and King over all things. He is the fulfillment of all that God intended for Israel and for the world. How can the portrait of Jesus in this book inform your understanding of God?

Connecting the Story Line

- Hebrews demonstrates the clear connections between the Old and New Testaments, united by the ultimate supremacy of Christ over all things.

- Hebrews argues that Jesus is superior to Moses and that the sacrifice of Christ is superior to the sacrifices listed in the Old Testament.

- Hebrews makes it clear that while Joshua led the Hebrew people into an earthly Promised Land, Christians await a heavenly Promised Land (the new heaven found in Revelation 21–22) that is far superior to any earthly home.

Day 39
The Letters of Peter and John

Setting Up the Story
Peter and John were both disciples of Jesus who learned from Him during His three years of ministry. When Jesus was crucified, they were left hurt and confused, unclear why the Messiah and King had just died and abandoned them. This perspective was radically changed by Christ's resurrection. Peter, for example, went from forcefully denying that he ever knew Jesus to boldly proclaiming Him as Lord in only a matter of days. Both Peter and John had firsthand encounters with the love, grace, and power of Jesus Christ. They understood who He was and the salvation He offered, and their letters are testaments to these facts.

If you have time, read the whole story: 1 Peter–3 John

A Chosen People
Read 1 Peter 2:9–12
What should our response to God's grace be?

_____

_____

_____

Sharing Christ's Attitude
Read 1 Peter 4:1–11
Why should Christians expect to suffer?

_____

_____

_____

Critical Observation

Peter argues that suffering because of Jesus is not a liability or a hindrance but rather an asset to our spiritual lives. He offers two primary reasons why we should embrace suffering: (1) The time is over for us to live for the desires of the body. When people seek to live for righteousness in this world, they stop simply living for their own pleasure and start living aware that they will give an account of their lives to Christ. (2) There is a reward that will follow obedience—eternal life. Ultimate redemption cannot be stopped, even if the world mistreats and persecutes believers.

THE TRUTH OF THE GOSPEL
Read 2 Peter 1:16–21
How does Peter know that the gospel is true?

_____

_____

_____

Insight

Christianity was not founded by a group of people who got together and decided to invent a new religion. Rather, it is based on what the apostles saw and heard—Jesus Christ dead and raised to life again.

THE LOVE OF THE FATHER
Read 1 John 3:1–6
What does it mean to you to be called a child of God?

_____

_____

_____

FAITH IN THE SON OF GOD
Read 1 John 5:1–5

According to John, how do we ultimately show love to God?

_____

_____

_____

Insight

A believer's love for God is expressed by his or her obedience, prompted by God's grace and in response to His love for us.

Judging by the sections you've read in this day's chapter, what ideas are most important to Peter and John?

_____

_____

_____

Take It Home

Both Peter and John talk quite a bit about love and the Christian community. They understand how important other believers can be to a Christian's life. God has equipped each of us with gifts that can help care for, love, and build up our community. Don't be a passive Christian. If you have time, talents, or money, consider joining a local church, where you can share the gifts God has given you.

Connecting the Story Line

- Both Peter and John are powerful testaments to the transformative work of Christ in a person's life. Their changed lives are evidence for the truth of Jesus' physical resurrection.

- The letters of these men are important documents for understanding the church, the world, and the place of suffering in the life of the Christian. They have helped believers for centuries with these difficult issues.

Day 40
The Book of Revelation

Setting Up the Story
Because of many persecutions, the church in the late first century was suffering. Many of the apostles had been martyred, and the apostle John had been arrested and placed in exile on the island of Patmos. The church needed spiritual, emotional, mental, and physical encouragement and stability to get them through their trials. John's letter—the recounting of a vision he had while in exile—is meant to encourage believers experiencing suffering by highlighting the supremacy of Christ, God's ultimate sovereignty, and the promise of future justice and restoration. It is a symbolic book that uses a number of different images to communicate different points, but each section further illustrates that throughout time, even in the midst of great trials, God will reign supreme.

If you have time, read the whole story: Revelation 1–22

John's Initial Vision
Read Revelation 1:9–20
What do the descriptions of Jesus suggest to you?

_____

_____

_____

_____

Critical Observation
It is important to recognize that John uses symbolic language throughout Revelation. For example, when he speaks of Christ as the Lamb or the Antichrist as a beast, he does not literally mean that they will look like animals.

Rather, he uses certain images to highlight important characteristics of Jesus and the Antichrist. This figurative language appears elsewhere in the Bible as well. For example, when Jesus calls Himself the bread of life (John 6:35), He does not literally mean that He is a piece of bread but rather that He ultimately sustains His followers like bread would sustain a hungry person.

THE SCROLL AND THE LAMB
Read Revelation 5:1–14
How does everyone respond to the Lamb?

_____

_____

_____

Critical Observation
In addition to the hope extended in this book, many scholars believe that Revelation offers insight into the timing of when Jesus will return to earth. Because of the cryptic writing of Revelation, there are more debates and viewpoints than can be summarized here. Most agree that while details of Christ's second coming are included in Revelation, John's primary purpose in writing is to provide hope to the struggling Christians of his day.

THE FALL OF BABYLON
Read Revelation 18:1–10
What is the message for Babylon?

_____

_____

_____

THE NEW HEAVEN AND EARTH
Read Revelation 21:1–5

In what ways are the problems created in the Garden of Eden finally resolved?

_____

_____

_____

In Revelation 21:2 John describes God and His followers as a husband and his bride. In what ways is this a powerful metaphor?

_____

_____

_____

Insight
The new heaven and earth have certain parallels to the Old Testament temple. The temple was the place in which God dwelt and was worshipped. There is no need for another temple, as the whole earth is where God lives and receives our worship. John makes this connection even more explicit later in the chapter (Revelation 21:22).

In what ways would the message of Revelation provide hope to Christians who are suffering?

_____

_____

_____

Take It Home

John's vision for the world God creates for His people is one of perfection from top to bottom. The original readers of the letter would have been given hope that the cruel and imperfect world that they endured was neither a reflection of God's vision for them nor the final result for humanity. We can share that hope in the midst of the pain and suffering that we experience, trusting that God's will and plan will eventually prevail. Though we cannot fully comprehend God's plan for the world, we can participate with Him in the restoration and work of His kingdom, living in eager anticipation of God's ultimate justice and reign. Do you have this hope for the future?

Connecting the Story Line

- Revelation is the only book of its kind in the New Testament. It is a type of writing known as apocalyptic literature, a term that comes from a Greek word that means to "reveal" or "unveil."

- John's prophetic visions are reflective of certain Old Testament themes, including the ultimate justice of God and His people's hope for restoration (see, for example, Isaiah 65–66).

Go Deeper with

THE QUICKNOTES
SIMPLIFIED BIBLE COMMENTARY SERIES